S0-BZO-648

Romantic Antics

Creative Ideas for Successful First Dates, Adventurous
Saturday Nights, and Playful Long Weekends

Joy and Kevin Decker

Adams Media Corporation
Avon, Massachusetts

Copyright ©2003, Joy and Kevin Decker. All rights reserved.
This book, or parts thereof, may not be reproduced in any form
without permission from the publisher; exceptions are made for
brief excerpts used in published reviews.

Published by
Adams Media Corporation
57 Littlefield Street, Avon MA 02322. U.S.A.
www.adamsmedia.com

ISBN: 1-58062-601-7

Printed in Canada.

J I H G F E D C B A

Library of Congress Cataloging-in-Publication Data
Decker, Kevin.
Romantic antics / Kevin Decker and Joy Decker.
p.   cm.
ISBN 1-58062-601-7
1. Dating (Social customs) 2. Man-woman relationships.
I. Decker, Joy. II. Title.
HQ801 .D438 2003
646.7'7--dc21
2002014286

Many of the designations used by manufacturers and sellers to distinguish their products are claimed as trademarks. Where those designations appear in this book and Adams Media was aware of a trademark claim, the designations have been printed with initial capital letters.

This publication is designed to provide accurate and authoritative information with regard to the subject matter covered. It is sold with the understanding that the publisher is not engaged in rendering legal, accounting, or other professional advice. If legal advice or other expert assistance is required, the services of a competent professional person should be sought.
—From a *Declaration of Principles* jointly adopted by a Committee of the American Bar Association and a Committee of Publishers and Associations

Cover photograph ©Steve Prezant/CORBIS.

This book is available at quantity discounts for bulk purchases.
For information, call 1-800-872-5627.

Dedication

To our son Benjamin.

Permissions

Quotes on pages 46–47 excerpted from *The Lazy Man's Way to Riches* by Richard Gilly Nixon, copyright © 1973 by Joe Karbo, © 1993 by Richard Gilly Nixon. Used by permission of Viking Penguin, a division of Penguin Putnam, Inc.

List on pages 57–58 reprinted with permission of Proflowers.com.

List on pages 59–60 reprinted with permission of Kentucky Fried Chicken.

"Today I am ninety-five" on page 123 excerpted from *Taking Control of Your Time and Your Life* by Dick Lohr, copyright © 1995 by CareerTrack publications. Reprinted by permission.

"Anchoring Rituals" on pages 126–127 from *Honey, I Want to Start My Own Business* by Azriela L. Jaffe. Copyright © 1996 by Azriela Jaffe. Reprinted by permission of HarperCollins Publishers, Inc.

Words and music on page 136 by John Lennon. © 1982 LENONO MUSIC. All rights controlled and administered by EMI Blackwood Music Inc. All Rights Reserved. International Copyright Secured. Used by permission.

List on page 214 reprinted with permission by Chuck DeLaney, Dean of the New York Institute of Photography.

Quiz on pages 247–248 reprinted with permission by Leslie Guttenberg. Printed as an article entitled "Coaching Your Partner," *Pros N' Hackers* magazine, June 2002.

Contents

Part Six: Special Occasions

Part Seven: Romantic Recipes

Introduction

Joy

~

KEVIN AND I BELIEVE that our lives and our relationship are blessed by God. We met in a bar in 1991, got married in 1995, and currently live in Fairfax, Virginia, with our two young children, Benjamin and Annika. That's the short version. A lot of what happened in between is written in the pages of this book.

Even before we were married we worked very hard to find ways to be romantic and loving with each other. We read books for romantic ideas and improving our relationship skills, talked with friends, read magazines, and took classes. We exercised our romantic muscles by surprising each other often and by finding creative ways to say "I love you."

We took an intensive three-month long communications class called Practical Applications of Intimate Relationship Skills (PAIRS). We discovered that we both were determined to have the kind of relationship that grows with us. One area of the class we focused on to help build romance skills was caring behaviors, those little things we do for each other that mean a lot.

Romance has been a constant in our relationship as it has evolved and deepened over the years. When we were married the logistics of living together changed but we made it a point to not take each other for granted. We still made time for romance and showing how much we cared.

Our lives changed profoundly when we found out that Joy was pregnant with our first child. We had to learn to keep the romance in our lives. Kevin knew from his volunteer work that the best way to learn was to teach. In 1997 we created InspirationPoint.com, our

Web site and e-zine, to teach visitors and readers to incorporate romance into their lives. As a result we learned much more about incorporating romance into our own lives.

We often send out a new romantic idea via e-mail to our subscribers, based on our own ideas and experiences. The ideas we send give readers specific things to do, skills to learn, and resources to get romantic.

Romantic Antics is a compilation of many of our ideas. It's loosely organized to cover the stages of a relationship from dating to courtship to marriage and beyond.

Our readers often share their romantic stories with us via e-mail. There are many romantics out there with creative, thoughtful, and loving ideas. We have included some of the best of these ideas as well.

Romance continues to keep our relationship alive. We hope you will use and share the ideas in this book to enhance your life and the lives of those you love.

Part One

Getting to Know You

"The First Day"

I wish I could remember the first day,
First hour, first moment of your meeting me;
If bright or dim the season, it might be
Summer or Winter for aught I can say;
So unrecorded did it slip away,
So blind was I to see and to foresee,
So dull to mark the budding of my tree
That would not blossom yet for many a May.
If only I could recollect it, such
A day of days! I let it come and go
As traceless as a thaw of bygone snow;
It seemed to mean so little, meant so much;
If only now I could recall that touch,
First touch of hand in hand—Did one but know!

Christina Rossetti, 1881

Our Meeting/First Date Story

Kevin

~

MY FRIEND ANDY INVITED ME to join him at a Saturday afternoon holiday concert. Carol, a friend of his, is a performer in the group and she got him tickets. I really enjoyed the show and happily crooned away during the sing-along portion. After the show the three of us went out for dinner. Carol said that some of the singers were headed out dancing later and I asked if I could come along.

At a nearby bar, Carol introduced me to some of her friends. We danced and talked for a while. A little later another singer came up and introduced herself as Joy. She was a pretty blond with a gregarious disposition and an engaging mind. I enjoyed talking with her, so I asked her to dance. Later, when we were talking again, I mentioned that I liked to cook but it's no fun for just one. Joy agreed heartily. I asked her if she'd like to cook for two. She was hesitant at first but agreed to make it a date.

We exchanged phone numbers and I called her the next week to set a date for dinner. Her busy performance schedule meant we had to wait awhile before our schedules could mesh.

Finally, the night of the date arrived. It was mid-January, and I was running late. I bounced up the walk and knocked on the door. A Brazilian flag hung in the window. I remembered that she mentioned she was born in Brazil. Joy looked great! I presented her with flowers and a bottle of wine. She loved the flowers and said the wine would go fine with dinner.

We moved to the kitchen where she was finishing her preparations. I asked if I could help but she said that everything was just about ready. Joy put the flowers in a vase and added them to the table she had set. She brought the last serving dish to the table and I held her chair as she sat down. We enjoyed a wonderful chicken curry dinner. After dinner I helped her clear the table and we had brownies topped with vanilla ice cream for dessert. I was very impressed.

Afterwards we moved to the sofa and discussed cooking, foreign travel, and many other topics. We talked for a long time that night. I called her the next day to thank her for a wonderful evening and to ask her out again. I was hooked!

To this day, Joy swears that my question about cooking was a "line" but it wasn't, just quick thinking on my part.

Our meeting may seem to have been the result of random chance, but we believe in serendipity. Opportunities to meet people abound. I took advantage of the opportunity by being flexible enough to join in last-minute plans and having the courage to step out of my comfort zone. After we met, I followed through by calling Joy several times while I waited for her schedule to clear.

Be flexible, have courage and perseverance, and you'll find yourself in the right place and time. Once you've turned that "chance" meeting into a first date, use the tips on the following page to make it a success!

First Date Tips

MEETING SOMEONE, and getting to know them, can be the hardest thing that some people will do. Others find it easier to get started but they may take even longer to really know their choice of mate. We've included some tips below to help with your first dates. Remember—even if you've been together awhile it doesn't mean you can't have a "first" date again!

Conversation Do's

- Maintain good eye contact—glancing about the room gives the impression that you're really not interested.
- Adopt a body posture that says you're alert and paying attention to what your date is saying.
- Ask questions and wait for a complete answer. Take your time to understand what was just said before asking an appropriate follow-up question. The most interesting people are those that are genuinely interested in you.

Conversation "Don'ts"

- Begin every sentence with "I"
- Tell jokes—they can offend easily
- Talk about money
- Talk about business
- Monopolize the conversation

Etiquette

Make the first overture. This is usually, but not necessarily, the guy's role. The tips that follow are written from a gentleman's perspective but can certainly apply to the ladies too.

Have a plan and a backup and a backup to the backup; weather changes, restaurants close, and movies get sold out.

Don't get stuck without something to do.

Dress accordingly and offer your date suggestions for appropriate dress.

Don't drink too much, if at all.

Go somewhere you can speak in conversational tones and spend time learning about each other. A walk in the park, a quiet corner of a restaurant, or a tour of the city offer plenty of opportunity for conversation.

Be positive and enthusiastic.

Escort her home—dropping her at the bus stop just doesn't make it.

Remain chaste and you'll appear classy and in control—it also adds a little mystery. Double dates or group dates can help with this.

Call her the next day. That's when you show that you are interested and want a second date.

Good Opening Lines

Generic

"Hello, my name is _____ . . . What's yours?"

"This place is really nice, isn't it?"

"You remind me of my _____ (friend, relative, or acquaintance)."

In a Grocery Store
- When he/she is looking at a particular food item, you can say:
  - I've tried that before and it was good (or it wasn't very good).
  - I've never tried that, is it any good?
- When he or she is reaching for an item on a high shelf or trying to lift something heavy, you can say: Can I help you with that?
- When you're standing in line look at the items he/she has put on the counter, and say:
  - Looks like you're eating healthy.
  - Looks like a decadent evening.
  - How would you cook that for two?
  - What's your favorite way to prepare those?

At the Library (Quietly, of Course)
- Do you like that author?
- I've read that and it's good (or bad, or so-so).

∼

Good opening lines are easy to come by if you pay attention to your surroundings and take a real interest in the person you wish to talk with.

Lightning and Thunder and Rain, Oh My!

Joy

~

SUMMER STORMS don't have to be known for interrupting your outdoor plans. When a summer thunderstorm kicks up, we open the curtains to the big window in the living room, sit on the couch facing it, and enjoy the sound and light show outside. The roaring booms that follow each brilliant strike resonate within us. It is a great opportunity to cuddle and snuggle together while watching the spectacular performance put on by Mother Nature.

Touch is important because it feels good and it's healthy for you. The feeling of snuggling together during the turbulence of a storm is comforting and a good way to spend some quality time together.

~

This idea is totally spontaneous, absolutely free, and a great way to make the most of a given situation. You've probably heard the old saying "When life deals you lemons, make lemonade." Ours was extra sweet!

Follow the Leader

Kevin

~

THOUGH THIS IS A GAME you may remember from your childhood days, you can turn it into an opportunity for romance as an adult. You are the leader. Your partner is the follower. The idea is to plan ahead of time to spend some time together without telling your mate what exactly you are going to do. When the time comes, your partner will "follow the leader", joining you in whatever activity you have planned.

Rules of the Game

1. Tell your partner you want to spend some time together, and you're going to plan the activity. All they have to do is show up.
2. Set a mutually agreeable date and period of time. We recommend no more than three to four hours.
3. Plan something you have always wanted to do, or that you know your partner would want to do. Pick something that is not abhorrent or offensive to your partner.
4. Inform your partner of any particular dress code needed.
5. When the time arrives, encourage your partner to relax and enjoy your time together, regardless of what you are doing. The partner does not get to protest or pout because he/she would rather be doing something else. You are in charge.
6. Fair's fair. After your follow the leader game, ask your

mate if he/she would like to take a turn. Reverse roles and let your partner take the romantic initiative.

Joy and I took turns at this game a couple of years ago. It was suggested to us as part of a communications course we were taking as a couple.

Joy asked me to be ready at 9:30 on a Saturday morning and to dress comfortably. Off we went into the springtime sunshine, headed for town. We drove past the monuments downtown and came to a stop in front of the Smithsonian Castle. Every year when the cherry blossoms are blooming the Smithsonian puts on a kite festival. They hold workshops that begin with a lecture on kites and give participants a chance to make their own kites. We made eddy's—traditional diamond-shaped kites with bows. We decorated our kites by creating designs on them that matched our interests. Joy's kite featured a musical note on it to represent her love of singing. My kite had a baseball diamond with a ball in the center, because I'm a big baseball fan. We actually flew the kites during the festival's competition. We didn't win any prizes but we still have the blue ribbons we received for participating.

Follow the leader is a lot of fun! Take turns creating some romantic and fun times for each other.

Fort Fixation

Kevin

~

ONE OF OUR EARLIEST DATES was an afternoon drive along the Potomac River in Virginia. We put the top down on Joy's Miata to enjoy the beautiful spring day. High clouds looked like cotton candy against a deep blue sky. The river was topped with small whitecaps whipped up by the breeze. There are a number of parking areas along the drive with scenic overlooks, and we pulled off the parkway at the site of an old fort named Ft. Marcy.

We walked along the old walls of the fort and found an old cannon, still on its wheels and carriage. Further along we found a comfortable spot hidden behind a wall and sat down to steal kisses from each other. It was very romantic!

We had a great time at Ft. Marcy and it established a fun precedent for us. Now whenever we're sightseeing and an old fort is nearby, we visit it looking for an out of the way place to cuddle and kiss. A couple of our favorites are the Royal Navy Dockyard in Bermuda, and San Juan's famous El Morro Fortress in Puerto Rico.

~

Find your local version of Ft. Marcy and take the time to develop your own Fort Fixation.

Aush, Madras Chicken, and Injera

Joy

∽

ONE OF THE THINGS I LOVE ABOUT KEVIN is his willingness to try something new. It's very romantic to share a dining adventure together. And the area in which we live provides plenty of ethnic food! Malaysian, Indian, Salvadoran, Peruvian, Moroccan, Ethiopian, Thai, Cuban, Afghani, you name it. It's a little bit like traveling to another country without leaving town.

On our second date Kevin took me to an Afghani restaurant. I had never tried their food before. The waiter gave us some recommendations and we started with aush, a tomato and pasta soup topped with yogurt and mint. Next came a light salad followed by lamb and chicken kabobs, sabsi (spiced spinach), and kadu (pureed pumpkin with a yogurt sauce). It was delicious. We returned to that restaurant many times, both for the food and the memories.

Another of our favorites is Indian food. Once I ordered a new dish, Madras Chicken, which turned out to be so spicy I couldn't eat it. Kevin, who has a much higher tolerance for hot, gallantly traded meals with me and we both enjoyed our dinners. That certainly made a romantic and memorable evening!

We ate Ethiopian food with our hands, in the traditional style. It was an intimate as well as delicious meal. The food came in large dishes to promote sharing. We tore off pieces of the sponge-like bread called injera, then dipped into the meat and vegetables. Sometimes we fed each other, and laughed as the sauce dripped down our chins.

~

Certain spices used in international foods
are considered to be aphrodisiacs. Ginger, cardamom,
nutmeg, or chilies could add some spice to your
relationship and your dinner. Try an ethnic food neither
one of you has had before. To start you off, we've
included the recipe for Madras Chicken on page 271.
We're sure you'll have a fun, hot, and romantic time!

Searching

Kevin

A VERY GOOD FRIEND OF MINE is still searching for the love of his life. He dates regularly, has gone on blind dates, and has even put an ad in the personals section of a local magazine. No luck yet.

I was thinking about him the other day as I sat through a seminar on recruiting and hiring. The speaker had just gone through a list of her ten tips on finding people to hire and I found that many of them applied to anyone that is searching for the "right" person. I picked the five that I feel are the most appropriate tips for finding your true love.

1. The search is a 24/7 task. You must be aware and alert to all the possible situations that can lead to meeting the right person. At your job, in the mall, and working out at the gym are all opportunities that can work equally well for meeting someone and starting a relationship.
2. You may have to kiss a lot of frogs to find your prince or princess charming. Of course you won't know they're frogs at first, but it probably won't take too long. Always remember to extricate yourself as gracefully as possible.
3. Figure out what your assets and liabilities are and work to maximize or minimize them as necessary. If you can sing, take her to a karaoke bar and serenade her in front of the crowd. If you work long hours and don't have much time for a social life, take a quick break during the day to phone him and make him laugh.

4. Trust your gut feeling. If it doesn't feel right, it probably isn't. We hope these tips help you on your search, and help my very good friend as well!

5. When all else fails, use a search firm. This can be expensive and may not work for you either. That's why we only recommend it as a last resort.

Make 'em Laugh

Joy

~

ROMANCE ISN'T ALWAYS SERIOUS BUSINESS. There is certainly a place for candles and tender words, but laughter is sometimes just what the doctor ordered. Kevin makes me laugh, and it's one of the things I love about him.

Once when I was home nursing a cold, he showed up in operating room scrubs and a toy stethoscope for a "house call"—he brought orange juice and a smile to my otherwise miserable day.

We once attended a marriage workshop and we were supposed to ask our partner, "What are you mad about?" I very seriously asked the question, and he replied in an equally serious tone, "about you!" I was rolling on the floor laughing—he really caught me off guard!

One time I called him at his office and he answered the ring in a very serious voice, "Yes, Mr. President." The fact that he works in Washington D.C. gave me pause, but he started giggling and I knew that I had the right number.

I often read a bit from *Reader's Digest* as I'm getting ready for bed, and he'll come in and say, "Read me a funny."

~

Make a conscious effort to make your partner laugh,

smile, giggle, or all of the above.

It's good for your heart and good for your soul.

Make laughter a part of your romantic relationship.

Part Two

Dating

"Meeting at Night"

The grey sea and the long black land;
And the yellow half-moon large and low;
And the startled little waves that leap
In fiery ringlets from their sleep,
As I gain the cove with pushing prow,
And quench its speed i' the slushy sand.

Then a mile of warm sea-scented beach;
Three fields to cross till a farm appears;
A tap at the pane, the quick sharp scratch
And blue spurt of a lighted match,
And a voice less loud, through its joys and fears,
Than the two hearts beating each to each!

Robert Browning

Dating

Kevin

~

ONCE YOU'VE GOTTEN PAST the initial stage of intoxicating attraction to someone it's time to narrow your focus and add depth to your relationship. In his book *Mars and Venus on a Date* John Gray talks about five stages of dating:

1. Attraction—Finding a potential partner
2. Uncertainty—Is this the right person for me?
3. Exclusivity—Removing the competition
4. Intimacy—Letting her experience the "Real You" with all your best and worst
5. Engagement—Certainty and celebration of your love for each other

Sometimes the transitions between stages can be subtle—others are much more obvious.

Joy and I had moved past the first stage and were going out together consistently but not exclusively. We were coming up on a weekend and on Saturday she was going on a trip with a bunch of coworkers. It was a teambuilding event that she'd planned for months in advance. I didn't realize it at the time but she transitioned us into stage three. "Is it okay if I start calling you my boyfriend?" she asked. I didn't have to consider the question long before I replied yes. She is engaging, intelligent, and very pretty and I wanted her to be my girlfriend exclusively.

We hope you'll use some of the ideas in this section to help you through all the stages of dating.

Kisses

*A kiss is a lovely trick designed by nature to stop
speech when words become superfluous.*

—Ingrid Bergman

Joy

DO YOU REMEMBER YOUR FIRST KISS? I remember when Kevin first kissed me. We were sitting on my couch on our first date talking when all of a sudden he leaned over and kissed me. It was very unexpected, and I wasn't at all sure I wanted to be kissed at that point. But that was then . . . now Kevin's kisses are welcome anytime!

Here is a list of great excuses to share a kiss:

- waiting at a red light
- riding the escalator
- leaving the house in the morning
- coming home at the end of the day
- leaning across the table at dinner
- going to bed
- watching a movie
- getting in the car
- getting out of the car
- just because

I remember once we were working hard on household chores when Kevin called to me, "Joy, come here please." I was busy, and impatiently ran up the stairs to find out what he wanted. He took me by the shoulders and gave me a long, soft, slow kiss that took my breath away. Then he said, "We can't have all work and no play." What a great reminder to take time out for the important things in life, like kissing your sweetheart!

Use all sorts of kisses:

- blowing kisses
- hand kisses
- butterfly kisses
- a peck on the check
- French kisses
- quick kisses
- slow kisses
- Hershey's kisses
- surreptitious kisses
- bold kisses

Build kissing into your daily activities.

Kiss your mate when they least expect it.

Make it a point to kiss at least three times

a day every day. We will!

Afternoon Tea

Joy

WHEN KEVIN INVITED ME on a date for 2 P.M. on a Saturday afternoon, I didn't know what to expect. It seemed an odd time for a date. He wouldn't tell me where we were going, only to dress nicely. I put on my favorite dress, braided my hair, and went to pick him up. I was driving my Miata then and loved to drive whenever I could. As we drove away from his house he still wouldn't tell me where we were going, he just gave general directions. Fortunately he's a good navigator and gives lots of warning about directions and turns. We drove into the city and stopped at one of the elegant hotels in Georgetown. Still wondering just what we were doing I followed him into the hotel. "We have reservations for tea" he told the doorman and got directions to the appropriate dining area. I was so surprised! I had never been to a tea before. The hotel was beautiful and the waiter prim and proper. Kevin ordered Earl Grey. I chose an orange spiced tea. We chatted over scones and cucumber sandwiches.

After we had our fill, a "gypsy" came by our table and read our palms. Although we were skeptical of the results, it was very entertaining.

A truly delightful and unforgettable date!

~

Spend an afternoon in style—take your mate to afternoon tea! Nicer hotels sometimes offer afternoon teas. Make sure you call to check days, times, and get a reservation. The setting is all white linen and silver, the hospitality is gracious, there might be a piano tinkling in the background. You can sit and chat with your loved one as you sip tea and nibble on finger sandwiches and buttered scones. Relax and enjoy an atmosphere of romance!

What's Romantic?

Joy

~

DO YOU KNOW WHAT IS ROMANTIC TO YOUR PARTNER? Can you mention a date from the past and have his/her face light up just from the memory? Does hearing a particular song, smelling a certain scent, or seeing a landmark make you smile and make your heart race? How do you create those memories in the one you love?

ASK!

Ask your partner to write down the scenario of the most romantic date he/she can remember. Be as specific as possible—including locations, attire, atmosphere, music, food, etc. The object is not to recreate the date just as it is written down, but to use the description as a basis for your dates in the future.

For example, if she likes Indian food, you could learn to make a few recipes at home (take a cooking class, maybe) and surprise her with a gourmet Indian meal one evening. If he enjoys the outdoors, plan a day hike together on a beautiful fall weekend.

~

The scenario provided by your significant other is just a starting point for your own imagination. Use this new information to create a special date that your sweetheart will remember for a long time.

Karaoke

Dennis W., Michigan

~

ONE NIGHT MY GIRLFRIEND, Denise, and I went to a place called Greektown in Detroit. We started out with a tour of one of the oldest churches in town then went to a Greek restaurant for dinner. After that we went to one of the fine pastry shops for dessert and cappuccino. We walked around the area a little bit and stopped at a karaoke bar. I used to sing professionally so I started the evening with "After the Lovin'" and ended it with "Falling in Love with You." There were stars in Denise's eyes and the crowd went crazy when I walked over to her, with mike in hand, and gave her a gentle kiss.

It was a perfect evening and a creative one for me, because when it comes to romance, I'm usually all thumbs.

~

Dennis took advantage of one of his strengths
to show his girlfriend how much she means to him.
Find a strength of your own and use it to your
advantage. Show your mate how much you care.

Kevin

Positive Reinforcement

Kevin

~

YOU ARE ATTRACTED TO YOUR PARTNER for a multitude of reasons. It could be the way they laugh, their sense of humor, or a special interest you share. Remember to tell your partner about these things. It will make him/her feel special, noticed, and desired by you.

Joy is beautiful and I don't mind telling her. She is smart and when she makes wise choices, I tell her about it. She is adventurous, she is thoughtful, and she is athletic. I'm sure that if you sit down and think about it, you can come up with a list of many positive things about your mate.

Positively reinforcing the good things about your mate and your relationship never gets old and always pays dividends. If I see Joy in an outfit that I like, I make sure to compliment her. When I buy her gifts I try to remember what colors and styles look good on her.

Your partner needs to know that she makes a difference to you—whether it's her clothes or making dinner or just walking at her pace when you're together.

~

Sit down now and come up with a list of ten specific

things you appreciate in the person you love—

then read it out loud to him or her.

Travel Evening

Joy

~

ONE OF THE MOST IMPORTANT INGREDIENTS for romance is creating the aura of a special place and time. A fantasy vacation is an adventure you can create right in your own home.

Talk with your partner about where he/she would like to go with an unlimited travel budget. Take a trip to the library, or surf the Net in order to learn more about that place—like culture, foods, dress, and lingo.

Using what you've learned, create an intimate fantasy evening recreating that place.

For example, if you wanted to spend a night in Tokyo:

- order in tempura or sushi
- eat with chopsticks, sitting on the floor
- wear bathrobes as kimonos and wear sandals
- have hot sake
- bow to each other

Or, if you'd like to spend a night in Rio:

- dress in the skimpiest clothes you have (it's very warm)
- prepare grilled meats or fowl (churrasco) with rice and beans
- play Brazilian music
- dance the samba or lambada

~

Use your imagination to create a fantasy
trip to romance! And don't forget to check
out our language reference on page 84 so you can say
"I love you" in the native language.

Five Stages

Kevin

～

THERE IS A FIVE-STAR RESTAURANT, The Inn at Little Washington, which is known around the world for its gourmet food. An engraved sign in the kitchen describes the restaurant's summary of the five stages of dining: Anticipation, Trepidation, Inspection, Fulfillment, and Evaluation.

These five stages are applicable for a romantic date too. For example, here's a recent date that Joy took me on:

First she invited me on a date for Saturday night. My level of anticipation built up as I waited for our night out (the timing for anticipation can be short, like a surprise party, or long, like planning a long vacation in the distant future).

I also had some trepidation about just what crazy thing Joy might have planned for the evening. Not a fearful trepidation but instead a quizzical apprehension. I was wondering as we pulled up to a video arcade.

I inspected the premises as we went inside and began laughing when I figured out what we were doing. Joy had booked us time at a Laser Tag facility! It's a digital version of a combat game that allows you to score points ("hits") without actually hitting someone or injuring them. I inspected the equipment they showed us as they explained the rules of the game.

At last, fulfillment! We had a great time running around the darkened room trying to catch each other with our laser weapons. After what seemed like an hour—but was actually only ten minutes—our game ended. We went back to the staging area and giggled and laughed about the adventure we had.

Afterward, we went to dinner and evaluated our game of tag. I'd have to say that it ranks very high on the fun scale—getting to share the experience with Joy gave it high marks on the romance scale, too.

~

Make a plan to work through the

five stages of a romantic date with your partner.

It will be a five-star experience!

Dinner at Home

Shelley B., Idaho

~

MY BOYFRIEND made our second date very distinctive.

We had planned an evening out with friends, so we could get acquainted slowly. There was a terrible storm, however, and power was cut off for several hours, so our friends had to cancel. His backup plan was to cook dinner at his house for me, and we were going to go dancing (one of my secret desires).

When I walked into his house, lovely music and warm candlelight filled the room. The furnishings were gorgeous. He took my coat and led me to the kitchen table. On the table was a bouquet of flowers, a bowl of strawberries, and a box of my favorite chocolates. There was champagne chilled on ice and a card with my name on it. The card featured a black and white photo of a little boy and girl, and a red rose! Inside my boyfriend wrote, "It is such a BIG world for these two small hearts to find each other! You have brought some wonderful color into my life just like this rose does to this card. Thank you for such a wonderful first week." I almost cried! What a precious thing to say!

We shared a glass of wine while listening to music. I sat on the kitchen counter while he cooked dinner for me. He put whipped cream on the strawberries and we fed them to each other, one by one. We tasted everything while it was cooking: Lobster, shrimp, baked potatoes, and vegetables. Our conversation was relaxed. We laughed, enjoyed each other's company, and connected on so many levels it was unbelievable!

~

Shelley's beau certainly knows how to make a good impression. He was flexible about arrangements and well prepared with a backup plan. He also set the stage for quite a romantic dinner at home with a variety of sensual pleasures. Taste, sight, touch, smell, and hearing were all covered in a most appealing way.

Be flexible, properly prepared, and remember the details on your next date. You'll make a very good impression, too.

Joy

Hot Air

Kevin

~

"The Balloonist's Prayer"

The winds have welcomed you with softness.
The sun has blessed you with his warm hands.
You have flown so high and so well
that God joined you in laughter and set you gently back
into the loving arms of Mother Earth.

Author unknown

~

A HOT AIR BALLOON RIDE can be a very romantic way to spend time together! You rise into the air slowly and quietly, view beautiful scenery from high in the air, land gently (most times), and then uncork a bottle of champagne to celebrate your successful flight.

Early one Saturday morning I surprised Joy with a trip to a local hot air balloon festival. When we arrived the local airfield was filled with more than a dozen balloons in myriad colors. Rides that day were tethered only but we spoke with a number of pilots about scheduling a flight at another time.

You can schedule an evening ride, but mornings are best, as

the weather conditions are optimum for lifting a balloon filled with hot air into the sky. The cost for a balloon flight runs around $150 dollars for about an hour in the air. Ballooning is at the mercy of the weather, so remember to be flexible if your flight has to be rescheduled. We've been rescheduled a number of times.

~

If the cost is outside of your budget, you can earn a ride by crewing for a flight team. You may want to visit a local festival to get a feel for ballooning before you take a ride. However you decide to do it, ballooning is a fun and romantic adventure for you to share.

Variations on Invitations

Kevin

~

TELLING SOMEONE YOU ADMIRE THEM and want to spend time with them is special. The standard method of calling them on the phone generally works, but if you really want to capture someone's attention, try something different:

Jigsaw Puzzle

One of Joy's passions in life is jigsaw puzzles. I sent her an easy, but romantic, personal puzzle without a picture. First create an invitation using a word processor. Use different font types, colors, and sizes to jumble the look of the invitation as much as possible. Then cut up the page into jigsaw puzzle-like pieces and deliver them to your partner. In no time at all Joy had my puzzle put together and was smiling even more. She gladly accepted my dinner invitation!

Cartoon

Copy a cartoon from a paper or book and modify the caption or add a new one to reflect your feelings. You can use a single cartoon to convey your love, make light of a funny situation, or ask for a date. Or, compile a series of cartoons for a romantic keepsake booklet.

I took a series of comics and copied them onto 8½ x 11 sheets of paper. I then added my own captions to the sheets.

I finished by punching holes in the paper and tying them together with ribbon. I had it delivered to Joy at her office. She loved it!

Crossword Puzzle

I faxed a homemade crossword puzzle to Joy at her office one day. Once she had solved it, she was instructed to fill in the blanks at the bottom of the sheet with words from the puzzle. It read, "Will you have dinner with me on Friday?" She was very surprised and impressed with the work that went into it. The fact that she loves puzzles and games made it even more special.

~

Use your imagination to create
a special invitation. I'm sure this
will start you on the road to a
wonderful date!

Paging Romance

Joy

~

KEVIN WEARS A PAGER FOR HIS JOB. He moves around a lot during the day so he's not always available by phone. If I really need to reach him, I can page him. Still, it's hard to convey a meaningful message with just a phone number. Do I need him to call back right away, or can it wait until he has a few minutes to chat? So we made up some numeric codes for phrases such as "Emergency" or "Call me when you can." We even have some codes that don't require a response, such as "I love you." Now I can page him with one of our codes just to let him know I'm thinking of him.

Here are some of our codes:

1	You're #1 in my life
99	I want to snuggle with you
25	Kisses
911	Emergency
411	Call me when you can
143	I love you (count the letters in each word)

~

Use our codes, or come up with your own.
I'm sure your sweetie will get the message.

Sunrise

Kevin

~

LONG BEFORE I MET JOY I spent five years in the Navy. For about one year I worked on the midnight-to-seven shift in the computer room aboard ship. One of the things I really enjoyed was ending my workday by walking outside to see the sunrise. The beautiful colors reflecting on the water were an inspiration. Back then I really wished that I had someone to share it with.

So after I met Joy, very early one Saturday morning, I called her for a surprise date. "Rise and shine, my love, I'll be by to pick you up in half an hour." The grunt on the other end of the line should have been a warning. I arrived promptly at 6 A.M. to hear Joy grumble "This better be worth it . . . "—it was. We had a delightful stroll by the waterfront downtown. I'd stopped for bagels and orange juice before picking Joy up. We found a park bench that gave us a great view of the sunrise and the Jefferson Memorial, and sat down to eat. We ate and talked and watched the world come alive as the sun came up. It was very romantic.

~

On the next gorgeous weekend, get yourself
and your mate up before the crack of dawn.
Go to a favorite park, lake, garden, path, or waterfront.
Hold hands and enjoy the dawning
of a new day together.

Onions

Joy

~

ONE OF THE WONDERFUL PERKS of dining as a couple is getting to share each other's meals. Kevin and I often begin negotiating as soon as we open the menus in a restaurant.

"What looks good to you?"

"I can't decide between the salmon and the pasta primavera."

"I'll order the pasta if you order the salmon."

"Deal!"

Or sometimes we don't deal, but when the meals arrive I look longingly at his dish until he offers me some. He can be very accommodating.

One evening we were trying out a new restaurant and we were at the salad bar. As I filled my plate I asked Kevin, "Are you going to have onions?" When he said yes, I added onions to my salad. A woman nearby overheard us and chuckled. Though she may have thought us crazy, I sure didn't want to be the only one with onion breath when we kissed later on!

~

Share your dinners and you may find that you share much more with your date!

Limo Ride

Joy

~

FOR A REALLY IMPRESSIVE DATE IDEA, rent a limousine!

I had just gotten a raise at work, and wanted to celebrate in a big way. I had never ridden in a limousine and thought it would be fun to surprise Kevin with one. I called around to check prices and I found a coupon in our local newspaper, so it wasn't as expensive as I had feared. I decided to go for it!

I arranged a date with Kevin and told him I would pick him up at his office at the end of the day. I had called the limousine service and arranged for them to pick up Kevin first, then come to my office to pick me up. I wish I could have seen Kevin's face when he realized the limo was for him.

That afternoon I could hardly concentrate at work, because I was anticipating the upcoming evening. As soon as I finished working, I quickly changed into a blouse and mini-skirt and hurried downstairs to wait in front of my office. And waited, and waited . . . finally a coworker came down with a message that Kevin had called from the limousine to tell me they were stuck in a big traffic jam, but they were on their way. Keep in mind, this was before the proliferation of cell phones so I thought it was pretty chic that he could call from the limo! I imagined Kevin sitting back and enjoying the ride instead of having to fight traffic himself—what a treat!

Soon Kevin arrived, still a little dazed by the surprise. He complimented my outfit and helped me into the car. It was huge inside! I felt very pampered as we drove to Haines Point, a park where there is a statue called "The Awakening"—it's a giant emerging from the ground. As we pulled up in front of the statue and got out, a little girl ran up to us and asked with wide eyes, "Are you famous?"

We strolled around the park and ate a picnic dinner I had brought while we watched the sunset over the Potomac. When the limo driver picked us up again, he asked, "Where to?" Kevin suggested a local bar not too far away and I suggested we go the long way around the heart of Washington, D.C. so we could enjoy the view of the monuments on our way there.

The bar Kevin suggested was one with a picture window looking onto the street so everyone could see us arrive in our posh transportation. We felt very elegant as we entered. We didn't have to worry about parking! We sipped our drinks and talked, and too soon it was time to head home. As the limo wound it's way back into town, we held hands and kissed on the back seat, no longer caring to view the scenery outside.

⌒

It was a lovely and memorable evening.
We think everyone should have a limo date
at least once in a lifetime.

Clue

Kevin

~

SOMETIMES THE ROMANCE is in the anticipation of a date as much as the date itself. Early in our relationship Joy asked me to dinner for the next Friday night. On Tuesday she left a message for me at work. "Clue number one for Friday night is that you need to feel adventurous."

I quickly called back for clue number two. A while later I received a call. "I'm sorry, sir, but you have reached your maximum clue limit for the day, please try again tomorrow." The next day, clue number two indicated the appropriate attire (blue jeans and the green polo shirt Joy likes). Clue number three on Thursday was about the time of the date.

On Friday morning there was no clue waiting so I called Joy. "Be patient," she teased.

Later I received a call from the reception desk. "Please come down and pick up your flowers." Clue number four was with the flowers. *Wait for me outside your office at the appropriate time this evening. Love, Joy.* When Joy picked me up she had a huge smile on her face that matched mine.

We went to my favorite park for a picnic dinner. Joy had spent Thursday evening testing new recipes and they were packed in her basket. We spread out a blanket, feasted on the delightful food she had prepared, walked around enjoying the sunshine until it waned, and then watched a glorious sunset together arm in arm.

Joy really surprised me with this date. The clue process was original and very creative; I really didn't know what to expect each day. She put a lot of thought into this date, built up my anticipation, and delivered with a marvelous finale.

~

Create your own clues to a date and deliver

them in a special way as Joy did.

It will certainly keep your mate guessing!

Road Trip

Kevin

JOY AND I RECENTLY TOOK A ROAD TRIP to Myrtle Beach. While road trips are a great way to spend quality time together, they can also quickly become monotonous. For those couples who enjoy the open road, we've found a number of ways to help us get to our destination in a great frame of mind.

Here are some tips for a fun, stress-free, and romantic road trip:

- books on tape
- cold drinks (non-alcoholic, of course)
- finger foods
- maps
- chocolate

We started out Saturday afternoon. I had confirmed our hotel reservations so we could take our time and not worry about losing our room if we got there late. That meant we had Saturday morning to pack and we also missed the usual Friday afternoon exodus from the city, which slows traffic to a crawl. Avoid crawling traffic, by all means!

With the car packed we headed off on our adventure. Joy pushed in the tape and we settled back with some pink lemonade, crackers, and cheese. Our favorite books on tape are mysteries that keep us guessing. In between tapes, we compare notes on who we think is the prime suspect. Pick a favorite genre or author, and have a backup in case your partner has already read it, or your car stereo eats the tape!

Later, we had a sumptuous dinner of tuna sandwiches and baby carrots along with cold sodas pulled from the cooler. It beats fast food any day!

I drive and Joy navigates. That division of labor works for us. Whatever you do, just make sure you have the right maps on hand, both regional and local. AAA can be helpful for this.

We spent about four hours on the road and arrived feeling tired, but not worn out. Four hours seems to be just the right amount of time for us. Try a variety of drive times to see what works for you and your mate.

We finished the second leg of our trip, and the second half of the book, on Sunday after a leisurely breakfast at the hotel. Again, it took just about four hours and we pulled up to the vacation office just after check-in time. We found our condo, unpacked, and started our romantic vacation right away.

The chocolates? The only acceptable payment for my navigator's work.

≈

Prepare for your next road trip with our checklist and help your vacation mindset get there sooner than ever before! Getting there is half the fun, right?

Pigmania

Kevin

~

JOY AND I LIKE TO PLAY LITTLE ROMANTIC GAMES with each other. My favorite is a modification of the game played in the SHMILY (See How Much I Love You) story. The goal of the game in the story was to write the word "shmily" in a surprise place for the other to find. As soon as it was found, it was the finder's turn to hide it once more.

When we first started dating Joy and I played a game from Milton Bradley called "Pass the Pigs." Joy thought the little inch-long pigs were so cute that when I saw some in a toy store I bought her a dozen for a gift.

On one of the pigs I drew a heart on one side and wrote "Joy" on the other. That pig turns up over and over again in the most unusual places. I've rigged it to pop out of a box of tissues, taped it to the earpiece on the phone, and squeezed it into a CD case. Sometimes it even finds its way down the back of Joy's shirt.

Joy has stashed the pig everywhere from my briefcase to behind the door of my tape player to the washing machine when unloading clean clothes (and a clean pig). One day I met a friend to play racquetball and when I unzipped the racquet case the pig popped out onto the court.

~

*Create your own little romantic game to
remind each other of your love.
The silly ones are the most fun!*

Salesmanship

Kevin

∼

I WAS AT THE END OF A VERY LONG marketing seminar, three days of twelve-hour sessions. We were discussing advertising and the critical components of an ad:

- a headline that seems personally written for the reader
- a promise of results from a product or service
- the advantages and disadvantages of the product
- identification of the seller
- a call to action

. . . when I thought I heard the instructor reading a love letter. Immediately I sat up in my chair and listened closely.

"Dear Betty," the instructor began, "I love you very much. I want to take care of you and our kids for the rest of your lives. There'll be good times and bad. But I'll try to do my best with what I've got. From time to time, I'll probably exasperate or annoy you. But I promise that you'll never be bored."

That's a good start for an ad. The headline speaks directly to the reader with a promise of the "service" to be delivered.

"I read somewhere that the contract for marriage is the only one that doesn't have a definite term—a point at which it ends or can be renewed. It just says ' . . . 'til Death do us part.' Well, I want you to know that, in our case, I'm satisfied with that arrangement. But, to be perfectly honest, I sometimes wish that we weren't married—so we'd both know, every day, that we were sharing our lives because we wanted to—not because we had to. All my love, Joe."

It's a wonderful love letter. The second half outlines the positives and negatives in the arrangement. The "seller" is identified after reassuring the "buyer" about the product. The only flaw may be no explicit call to action.

I've never forgotten that class. I later found that the instructor was reading from the "How to Write Successful Ads" chapter of *The Lazy Man's Way to Riches* by Joe Karbo. It was out of print for a while but an updated version by Richard G. Nixon is now available. I recently got my own copy and keep it to remind me of the power of an ad, and a love letter.

~

Write your sweetie a love letter today!

Quotes excerpted from *The Lazy Man's Way to Riches* by Richard Gilly Nixon, copyright © 1973 by Joe Karbo, © 1993 by Richard Gilly Nixon. Used by permission of Viking Penguin, a division of Penguin Putnam, Inc.

Mystery Getaway Weekend

Joy

~

A VERY CLASSIC AND ROMANTIC IDEA for some intimate time away is the mystery getaway weekend.

Kevin and I had been working hard at the office and we needed a break so I planned a mystery getaway weekend for us. On the designated Saturday I picked him up in my bright blue Miata and off we went.

It was a gorgeous afternoon in early fall, and we put the top down to enjoy the weather and the scenery as we drove into the countryside. We headed west toward the Blue Ridge mountains. We turned off the interstate and onto quiet country roads shaded by trees.

As we approached the bed & breakfast where we had reservations, I could hardly wait! We followed the driveway to the top of the hill and were warmly greeted by our hosts. The bedroom was lovely and comfortable, the bath was luxurious, and we enjoyed the gourmet meals and the company of another couple staying there. We stayed two nights and spent a whole day sightseeing along the Blue Ridge Parkway. We relaxed and enjoyed our time together.

The key for a great getaway weekend is in the planning:

- Make sure you've cleared a date and time; Kevin once cleared my time off with my boss for a surprise he planned.
- Know what your mode of transportation is; car, train, or plane can all be made romantic.

- Have a definite place to stay with confirmed reservations; nothing is worse than finding only "No Vacancy" signs at your destination
- Plan meals and make reservations if needed.

Bed & breakfasts can be luxurious and expensive, but there are other options:

State Parks: State Parks are fairly inexpensive, and usually offer a variety of accommodations, such as campgrounds, cabins, and lodge rooms. They often have spectacular scenery. We once stayed at Cacapon state park in West Virginia, which has a first-class golf course, a lakeside beach, horseback riding, and plenty of hiking trails.

Off-season beach weekend: I love the ocean in all kinds of weather. It may not be warm enough for swimming, but the rates are reasonable and you'll have the beach to yourselves for long walks. Go shopping, warm up with some clam chowder, and snuggle together.

Budget getaway: Stay home. Tell everyone you're going out of town, unplug the phone and pretend you're a tourist. Go sightseeing in your own town. Take a bubble bath when you get home. Splurge on dinner at a nice restaurant. Spend Sunday morning in bed reading the paper and doing the crossword puzzle together.

～

Any way you do it, a getaway weekend
is a great way to recharge with your mate!

Quick Long-Distance Ideas

Joy

~

MANY VISITORS TO OUR WEB SITE write to us about their long distance relationships (LDRs). Being apart can be particularly stressful on a relationship, yet there are opportunities for romance, too.

Here are some quick, easy, and inexpensive ideas that were sent to us by visitors to our Web site. Try not to let distance interfere with your relationship. Use these ideas to show your romantic side even when you are apart

Box of Cards

If you're going to be gone for a while, buy or make enough cards so that you have one for each day that you're gone. Date the envelopes for each day and write a little note in the card for that day. Put all the notes in a special gift-wrapped box and give it to your sweetheart before you leave. While you're apart, he/she can open and read a daily personal, romantic note from you.

Night Under the Stars

Lying together on a blanket in the middle of a field staring up at the stars in the night sky can be very romantic. Create your own version of a night under the stars. Get a piece of black poster board and attach a silk flower, some glow in the dark stars, a piece of blanket, and a picture of the two of you. Send it to your honey with a note that says, "Redeem this poster for a real night under the stars as soon as I return, until then know that I'm thinking about you each time the stars come out."

Journal of Romance

Buy or make yourself a small notebook. On the cover place one of your favorite pictures. Each day use it to journal your thoughts, feelings, or activities, especially those which relate to your mate. When the pages are full, send it to him/her. Sharing your days will bring you close together even when you're apart.

Movie Time

When you know that you are going to be separated by one or more time zones, suggest that you both watch a romantic movie at the same time, taking into account the time difference. When the couple in the movie kisses, celebrate by toasting with a similar wine or other beverage. Later, call and talk about what you liked about the movie.

Personalized Phone Card

Joy

~

HERE IS A GREAT LONG-DISTANCE GIFT: A phone card. You know, those ubiquitous prepaid phone cards that have a certain number of minutes you can use to talk long-distance? I found a Web site from which you can order a personalized version with your photo on the front. I chose one of Kevin's favorite photos of me, and sent it off with the order. Soon I received by return mail a phone card with my picture on it!

Now whenever he's gone he'll have that picture to remind him of me, and he can use the card to call me right away and tell me how much he misses me.

~

Stay in touch with your mate with a personalized

phone card. Check the Appendix for some

Web sites that can help you get your

own special card.

LDR Video

Kevin

JOY AND I SUFFERED through a temporary long-distance relationship (LDR) when she was sent to a fifteen-week training
program in another state. At first we called each other every
day, then we got the first phone bill. Ugh. However, Joy came
up with a very creative way to let me know that she was thinking
of me.

One day a package arrived for me from Joy. The package
held a videotape and a note, which instructed me to get myself a
drink, some snacks, and sit down to watch the tape. At first the
screen was dark. I could hear her breathing lightly, then her
alarm clock went off. After some rustling a light clicked on and
Joy looked at the camera and said, "Good morning, love, I
wanted you to spend the day with me."

The next scene was Joy in workout attire on her NordicTrak,
telling me she was trying to keep fit while she was away. Next she
was in her robe ironing her clothes for the day. "I know you like
this outfit, I picked it just for today," she said.

She showed me her breakfast and then we were in her car.
"Off we go to work!" she said as she turned on the radio. Then
the video showed clips of her classroom and a few of her class-
mates. After work and back at her apartment Joy chatted to me
about her classes that day as she prepared a dinner of spaghetti
and garlic bread. She showed me the laptop she was using to do
her homework. The last thing on the tape was "Good night, dear,
sweet dreams" along with a big hug and kiss, then the screen
went dark.

The tape helped us connect on a level beyond flowers, a card, or even a phone call. I really felt like I'd been a part of Joy's day. I'll treasure that tape always.

~

You can create your own video to help you make it through your LDR. Joy borrowed a video camera and bought a blank videotape. It may help you to prepare a simple script of your day. Use the video to tell your mate that you love and miss him or her and are thinking about him or her all day.

Message in a Bottle

Key L., Massachusetts

~

HERE IS A UNIQUE IDEA for someone in a long distance relationship: Age a piece of parchment paper by using a brewed teabag and rubbing it onto the paper. Singe the edges of the paper for added effect. Write a love story or note as if you are away at sea and are desperate to express your love. You might use the poem "Meeting at Night" which is included in this book. Calligraphy is a nice touch if you know how. On the back of your letter write the following message:

If you find this bottle, please forward it to my love
[list your sweetie's name and address]

Roll the paper tightly around a pencil and remove the pencil, tie it with light, tattered twine, and drop into a wine bottle that you've removed all the labels from and cleaned. Cork the bottle and pack it in a box.

Have a friend place it outside your love's door, or use a mailing service such as Mail Boxes Etc., or Federal Express that will forward your message to your beloved.

~

Having spent five years in the navy and much of it aboard ship at sea this idea hit home for me. I really like the tip to age the parchment with a used tea bag. Let your mate uncork your love with a message in a bottle.

Kevin

Bon Voyage Bag

Kevin

~

I WAS HEADED TO CLEVELAND for a business trip and Joy had agreed to drop me off at the airport. As I was unloading the trunk at the terminal she reached into the back seat and pulled out a bag and said, "Bon Voyage!"

Joy had made a goody bag for my trip. It had snacks and a deck of cards for playing solitaire, toiletries, magazines to read, and a romantic homemade card. I was so surprised! I dislike airplane travel and the diversions she gave me helped me to pass the time.

The flight was over before I knew it and I knew that I had Joy to thank for an enjoyable plane ride. She had even thoughtfully included another magazine for the trip back.

Prepare a Bon Voyage bag for your sweetheart for their next business trip.

Bon Voyage goodies can include:

- candy
- a deck of cards
- magazines
- love notes
- gum
- a current newspaper
- a phone card
- a box of his/her favorite juice or a can of soda

This thoughtful and practical gift will really be appreciated!

Corporate Sponsored Romance

Kevin

~

YES, CORPORATE AMERICA SPONSORS just about everything these days—even romance. Look around and you'll see special advertisements, sales, and contests for romantics. Hallmark sponsored the "Queen of Hearts/ King of Hearts Countdown." The contests always offer great prizes but if you look closer you'll often find ideas for romance. The Proflowers.com "Staying Power" promotion provided ten tips for keeping romance alive all year long:

1. **Be Creative:** Music has taught us that nothing is more romantic than the human mind. Use your imagination to turn ordinary experiences into extraordinary delights. Turn an ordinary beach bonfire into a romantic experience by digging out sand furniture for you and your lovely to lounge on beneath the stars.
2. **Be Young At Heart:** Part of the joy of being a child is experiencing each moment as a first and when it comes to romance, there's nothing like being the first—the first kiss, the first date—firsts are very important. A summer rain shower is the perfect excuse to visit an empty playground, splash in the puddles and push your sweetie on a swing.
3. **Be Fun:** Trust us, if you're not having fun—it isn't romantic. What's more fun then a tandem bike ride to a

secluded picnic? Bring your favorite toys and games and add a few romantic twists to the rules. How about a heated game of Truth or Dare?

4. **Be Spontaneous:** Romance is spontaneous and uncontrollable, that's what makes it so darn fun! Ask your lover to dance with you someplace unexpected like a park, restaurant, or street corner. All you need is a little music and their body next to yours.

5. **Be Adventurous:** Love is an adventure and should be treated as such. Road trips are the perfect way to add a little adventure.

6. **Be Sincere:** You don't have to be a Casanova to realize the best romances are rooted in sincerity and trust. It's the only way to really open yourself to another person.

7. **Be Unique:** Each and every romance is unique in its own way but it helps to add a touch of your own personality. Don't just serve breakfast in bed—make sure they have reason to stay there for lunch, dinner, and dessert as well.

8. **Be in the Moment:** Yeah, there's nothing wrong with working the "kinks" out with someone you love. A sensual body massage with scented oils is the perfect cure for an attack of the late night "kinks." Remember romance is about having fun together.

9. **Be Sensual:** Sensuality is a state-of-mind, an intimate connection between two people. Of course, a piping hot bubble bath peppered with rose petals and a foot rub goes a long ways, too.

10. **Be Just the Way You Are:** You can't be anything to anyone if you can't be yourself.

List reprinted with permission of Proflowers.com.

One of our favorite contests was the Kentucky Fried Chicken "Buckets of Love" contest. They selected the top eleven ideas for a successful marriage submitted by couples celebrating their fortieth wedding anniversary. They selected forty years to tie in with their fortieth year in business. We are very happy that "Plenty of Romance" made the list.

While KFC will never reveal the famous eleven secret herbs and spices in its chicken, the contest judges zeroed in on these eleven ingredients for a successful marriage.

1. **Selectively poor memory**—Grand-prize winners Judy and Marv Rifkin of Agoura Hills, California, write, "I can't remember what he looked like with all his hair and teeth, and he can't remember what I looked like when I could fit into my wedding gown. We don't remember how small our first apartment was, but we do remember how much fun we had there." For all that they do remember and don't remember, the Rifkins boast, "We sure remember why we got married forty years ago in the first place!"

2. **Give-and-take**—Don and Netta Prosise of Phoenix advise "doing what the other one wants to do part of the time, even if it's not your cup of tea."

3. **Sense of humor**—For Cliff and Peggy Duck of Hacienda Heights, California, humor is an essential ingredient in marriage.

4. **Good communication**—Lee and Joyce Gassert from Placentia, California, set aside a night each week for a date where the two of them can talk.

5. **Hugs and kisses**—Roland Schnabel of Tampa always gives his wife Jean a kiss when he comes home from work.

6. **Trust**—Gleon and Connie O'Kane from Princeville, Illinois, share trust "in each other's thoughts, words,

plans, commitments, and actions."

7. **Loving children**—John and Peggy LaMure of Madisonville, Kentucky, have five children. And they joke that "whoever left the marriage had to take all five of them."

8. **Plenty of romance**—For Walter and Ann Warren of Dorchester, Massachusetts, the romance remains as strong as when they met while dancing many years ago.

9. **Faith**—"Our marriage is based on our love for God and for each other," according to Paul and Mary Goin of Galion, Ohio.

10. **Patience**—Wayne and Ruth Neilson from West Jordan, Utah, say "if you have patience, everything else will come together."

11. **Teamwork**—"We share every decision from child rearing to picking out carpet," admit Bill and Becky Sharp from Hilton Head, South Carolina.

~

Keep your eyes open for more sponsorship

of romance by corporate America.

You never know what you might learn, or win!

List reprinted with permission of Kentucky Fried Chicken.

Top Ten Romantic Movies
Kevin

~

THE AMERICAN FILM INSTITUTE released a list of the Top 100 Love Stories of the last 100 years. They started with 400 nominations and whittled it down to 100. Joy and I have our list, too. It started as a top ten list, but it grows all the time. Our list goes all the way back to the 1930s and includes Bogart, Gable, Grant, Douglass, Bergman, Hepburn, Benning, and Ryan. We're using our list to build a library of romantic movies. Although some of our favorites aren't on the AFI list these are movies that we both enjoy, find romantic, and can watch again and again. Start building your personal list of romantic movies. You'll always know what to look for in the video store for an evening of romance.

- *Casablanca* (1942)
- *The American President* (1995)
- *The Big Easy* (1987)
- *Bull Durham* (1988)
- *Charade* (1963)
- *Chocolat* (2000)
- *Father Goose* (1964)
- *Ghost* (1990)
- *The Goodbye Girl* (1977)
- *It Happened One Night* (1934)
- *L.A. Story* (1991)
- *The Princess Bride* (1987)
- *Sabrina* (1954)
- *Sleepless in Seattle* (1993)
- *To Catch a Thief* (1955)
- *Princess Carabou* (1994)

Part Three

Courtship

"How Do I Love Thee?"

How do I love thee? Let me count the ways.
I love thee to the depth and breadth and height
My soul can reach, when feeling out of sight
For the ends of Being and ideal Grace.
I love thee to the level of every day's
Most quiet need, by sun and candlelight.
I love thee freely, as men strive for Right;
I love thee purely, as they turn from Praise.
I love thee with the passion put to use
In my old griefs, and with my childhood's faith.
I love thee with a love I seemed to lose
With my lost saints,—I love thee with the breath,
Smiles, tears, of all my life!—and, if God choose,
I shall but love thee better after death.

Elizabeth Barrett Browning

Our Falling in Love Story

Joy

DINNER AND A MOVIE is a great traditional date combination. You can't go wrong with it, and it's a good bet if you don't know the other person well. After two months of traditional dating, however, Kevin was ready to try mixing things up.

Kevin didn't tell me where we were going that evening, just that he'd pick me up at six and to wear something nice. I was astonished when we arrived at the Kennedy Center, the premiere cultural center of Washington D.C. I knew then I was in for a special evening. We entered the hall and walked to the Opera House, through the crowd of elegantly dressed ladies and gentlemen. When I realized we were going to a ballet performance, I was really impressed with Kevin and his cultural taste.

We were both starving as we left the ballet, and Kevin said, "I know just the restaurant." Soon we were feasting on a slab of ribs at a local Memphis-style barbecue pit. The juxtaposition of ballet and barbecue told me that Kevin has a unique perspective on life and how to enjoy it. Although we were definitely overdressed for the ambiance and the music (a great collection of blues tunes) wasn't exactly classical, the food was excellent. We finished our meal sharing a creamy banana pudding. It was a great contrast to the first part of the evening.

Later that night Kevin took me home and left me with a kiss to savor the memories of the evening. I thought about how he had planned the evening so carefully and how much fun we had together, and I knew that I was in love with him. It was March 20, 1992.

Kevin and I still celebrate March 20th as the date I fell in love with him.

The Romantic
Relationship Riddle
Joy
~

WHAT IS THE CORRECT ANSWER to Kevin's question:

Honey, when I return from my trip, where will you pick me up at the airport?

    a. at the airline baggage claim, or
    b. at the curb outside?

The correct answer is a hidden answer:

    c. sweetheart, I'll meet you at the gate!

Sometimes the most romantic thing is to go an extra step for your mate.

I was meeting Kevin at the airport and wanted to welcome him home with more than just a kiss and an "I missed you." I was browsing through our romance bookshelf looking for an idea when I found a book of classic romantic poetry. Aha, just the thing! I typed one of my favorite poems on the computer. It's Elizabeth Barrett Browning's "How Do I Love Thee?"

It's an oldie and a goodie. I played with the fonts to find just the right look for the text, and printed it out on a piece of parchment paper. Then I rolled it up into a scroll and tied a thin red ribbon around it for added effect. On the way to the airport I stopped at a flower shop and chose a single red rose. I arrived early and had to wait quite awhile before his plane arrived. I watched it pull into the gate, and I waited at the end of the jetway as lots of people came off the plane. Finally I saw Kevin; he was the last person to exit and was loaded down with his bags. I had the biggest grin as I waited for him to see me.

He looked exhausted but when he saw me his face brightened. He dropped his bags and I gave him a big hug and a kiss. Then I handed him his flower and the scroll. A broad smile appeared and he seemed to relax. It was just the response I was hoping for.

~

There are so many opportunities in life to make your mate feel special and loved. Make sure you spend the extra effort and take advantage of all you can.

Caring Behavior

Joy

≈

ONE OF THE BEST WAYS to show you care is to do the things your mate considers to be caring. How do you know? *Ask!* Develop a top ten list of each of the caring behaviors you value most and ask your partner to do the same. Try to do at least two items from the list each day for your partner.

Joy's List

1. Hold my hand in public.
2. Give me a variety of kisses.
3. Listen to me.
4. Call me to say hi.
5. Surprise me.
6. Brush my hair.
7. Hug me.
8. Compliment me.
9. Hold me when I'm sad and crying.
10. Tell me you love me.

Kevin's List

1. Hug me.
2. Kiss me.
3. Give me cards.
4. Make dinner for me.

5. Give me a wink and a smile.
6. Cuddle with me.
7. Tell me I'm wanted.
8. Wash my hair.
9. Play with my hair.
10. Call me and make me laugh.

We hope these lists have given you a place to start.

How Well Do You Know Your Partner?

Joy
⁓

BEING ROMANTIC MEANS knowing what your mate likes, so you can choose appealing gifts and activities. The thought that goes into these choices makes them more meaningful and romantic.

For example, when we were first dating, Kevin found out that my favorite movie was *The Court Jester*, with Danny Kaye. I rented it once and we watched it together. The next Christmas, guess what was under the tree for me? He had remembered, and now I own a copy of *The Court Jester*, which I have enjoyed watching over and over again.

Use the checklist below to find out how much you know about your significant other. Once you know what the right answers are, keep your partner's list in a safe place and refer to it often. Choose one and be romantic in your partner's favorite way!

My Partner's Favorite Things

favorite flower:_____

favorite poet/poem:_____

favorite sport/team: _____

favorite ice cream: _____

My Partner's Favorite Things (continued)

favorite color: _____

favorite song/singer: _____

favorite movie: _____

clothing sizes: _____

favorite actor: _____

first section he or she reads in the paper: _____

favorite magazine: _____

favorite dinner: _____

favorite breakfast: _____

favorite lunch: _____

favorite dessert: _____

birth date: _____

birthplace: _____

favorite author/book: _____

dream vacation spot: _____

favorite restaurant: _____

favorite comic strip: _____

favorite wine/beverage: _____

favorite cheese: _____

favorite scent/perfume/aftershave/cologne: _____

Where Am I?

Kevin

~

RESET YOUR MENTAL MAP for romance! Most of us travel between home and work and the grocery store with only an occasional thought on where to find something special for our loved one.

Do you know where the closest:

- Greeting card store is? A loving card often means the most when it's sent on an ordinary day.
- Flower shop is? When was the last time you stopped for flowers on the way home from work?
- Video rental shop is? Rent a romantic video and watch it together.
- Toy store is? Fun isn't just for children.
- Bookstore is? Who is your mate's favorite author?

Get to know each one of these in relation to your home and your office. You should be a regular customer at each of these businesses.

~

Your assignment is to find, visit, and use each of these places. Reset your mental map for romance and see where it takes you.

Flowers

Kevin

~

FLOWERS RATE VERY, VERY HIGH on the gift scale for women and men alike. Some guys probably won't admit it but we get a kick out of receiving flowers. The fragrance and beauty of flowers appeal to the senses, and they also convey the message that someone special is thinking of you.

I love it when Joy sends me flowers at the office and all the women make a fuss over me. I tell them about what a wonderful wife I have.

Here are a few simple ways to cherish your love with flowers:

- Personally deliver a single red rose to the door of your loved one. This can be the start of a romantic date or an unexpected visit. Hand it to them with the words, "Here is a token of my love."
- I have been able to get roses at a discount by visiting the florist and asking for flowers before they're arranged or even taken out of the delivery containers. These are just what you want to use to cover the floor with rose petals. You can sprinkle them around the room and have a romantic dinner with candles and soft music. Or you can leave a trail through the house leading to a warm bath.
- Put together a bouquet with a special meaning. Read the list that follows to find out flower meanings, and choose the arrangement that best fits your thoughts. Include a love note that explains the special arrangement you have created. Your thoughtfulness will be even more appreciated than the flowers themselves!

A friend of ours suggested this charming idea: sneak into her house and make a trail of Hershey's kisses from her front door to her bathroom. Hang a dozen roses from the showerhead. Leave a note that reads, "I kiss the ground you walk on and shower you with roses."

As you probably know, flowers and their colors have special meanings and we've included a list below.

Flower	Meaning
Allium	Good fortune
Amaryllis	Suggests pride
Anemone	Abandonment
Anthurium	Intense attraction
Aster	Beginnings
Batchelor's Button	Solitude
Bird-of-Paradise	Strange and wonderful
Buttercup	Childishness
Camellia	Honest excellence
Chrysanthemum	Hope
Crocus	Youthful gladness
Daffodil	Chivalry
Dahlia	Instability
Daisy	Innocence
Delphinium	Swiftness and light
Dogwood	Endurance
Forget-me-not	Keepsake
Freesia	Calm
Gardenia	Feminine grace

Flower	Meaning
Gerbera	Purity
Gladiolus	Natural grace
Heliotrope	Devotion
Hibiscus	Seize the opportunity
Hollyhock	Fertility
Honeysuckle	The bonds of love
Hyacinth	Young love
Hydrangea	Boasting
Iris	A message
Jasmine	Good luck
Lavender	Lack of trust
Lilac	Sadness
Lily	Innocence
Magnolia	Expresses dignity
Marigold	Bittersweet
Mimosa	Sensitivity
Narcissus	Egotism
Nasturtium	Jest
Orchid	Ecstasy
Pansy	Lovers' thoughts
Peony	Keep a secret
Periwinkle	Promise
Plumeria	Love while absent
Pomegranate	Unspoken desire
Poppy	Wonder of dreams
Primrose	Hope
Protea	Challenge of desire

Flower	Meaning
Queen Anne's Lace	Self-reliance
Quince	Temptation
Ranunculus	Charm
Red Heather	Passion
Red Rose	Passionate love
Rosemary	Remembrance
Snapdragon	Impetuous
Sunflower	Power
Sweet Pea	Lasting pleasure
Tulip	Declare your love
Violet	Faithfulness
Water Lily	Perfect beauty
White Heather	Protection from rash acts
White Rose	Purity
Wisteria	Obedience
Yellow Rose	Jealousy
Zinnia	Absence

Pamper on a Budget

Kevin

~

I WANTED TO DO something special for Joy, so I spoke with a woman at the local full-service beauty salon about a gift certificate. *Ouch*! The cost exceeded my budget. After some creative thinking, I decided I could duplicate the luxury of a salon for Joy in her very own home.

I made a date with her for dinner and said that I was in charge of all preparations and instructed her to be "not ready" two hours early.

Before going to Joy's I went to the pharmacy and picked up bubble bath, shampoo, and bright red nail polish. I showed up at her place with my clothes packed in a bag and the second bag with all the fixings

When I arrived, I gave her the bottle of bubble bath and sent her off to the bathroom to begin. She ran a very hot bath and got in. While she soaked, I went to her closet and selected her short black dress—it's my favorite, and she looks stunning in it. I also laid out all the accessories she would need. Joy called me when she was ready. I gave her a shampoo, deep conditioning, and a rinse. By the time I was finished, she was feeling quite relaxed.

When she emerged wrapped in her terry cloth robe, I sat her down and painted her nails red. All twenty of them! This was a hoot as I'd never done it before and it's much harder than it looks. (Hint: Bring some nail polish remover, too!) While the polish dried I massaged her neck and shoulders.

Once her spa treatment was complete, we went to dinner. Joy looked great. It's amazing how you can tell when someone is relaxed and comfortable. What a wonderful evening!

∼

Pamper your date and make her feel

and look beautiful! (If your date is a man,

you can skip the nail polish!)

Ice Cold Licks!

Kevin

∼

JULY MEANS SUMMER and summer is hot. What better way to chill out and cool off than with ice cream? It just so happens that July is National Ice Cream Month! So celebrate! There are lots of ways to enjoy ice cream together:

- Share licks of an ice cream cone.
- Buy a pint and feed it to each other.
- Order an ice cream cake with a dedication to the one you love inscribed on top.
- Have a chocolate double dipper at Dairy Queen. Boy, that brings back memories!
- Make a homemade deluxe banana split with all the trimmings, and serve with two spoons!
- How about a root beer float while sitting at the counter of an old-fashioned soda fountain?
- Have a make-your-own-sundae party. Provide at least three kinds of ice cream, and all sorts of toppings.

Order a six-pack or even a twelve-pack of Ben & Jerry's. Imagine a dozen times the cold delights. They'll pack your Ben & Jerry's in dry ice and deliver it to your door.

∼

Make plans now to celebrate ice cream
month with your honey!

Fond of Fondue

Kevin

~

IT'S AMAZING TO ME the different varieties of cheese and ways to prepare it. A rich and creamy macaroni and cheese is comfort food—Mexican Chili con queso, Greek saganaki, or an Indian paneer with vegetables all spell adventure.

Joy, however, loves fondue. The allure of fondue is the atmosphere of food, drink, and talk it creates.

As we entered the restaurant and took our seats I thought "The setting is certainly right." The lights were low, the seats comfortable, and light jazz played in the background. I was surprised to learn that fondue wasn't just about cheese.

Our appetizer was served with vegetables, apples, and three kinds of bread for dipping. We soon figured out that the fondue fork needs a firm hold on your food before you put it in the fondue pot, or else the food is likely to fall off and disappear.

The main course was a combination of meats and vegetables in bite sized cubes for us to simmer in a hot broth. We cooked, talked, ate, and kissed. What a wonderful way to enjoy a meal!

Dessert was sinful—fresh fruit to dip in a chocolate sauce.

~

The next time you want a special dinner treat,

consider fondue—it's tasty and romantic.

Paying Tolls

Kevin

⁓

LATELY IT SEEMS that there are more and more tolls on stairways and escalators. What's funny about them is that Joy always has to pay when going down, and I always have to pay when going up. It doesn't matter what city, state, or even country we're in.

No, the government hasn't found a new way to collect more money from us. Let me explain, Joy is about a foot shorter than I and when she stands on the nine inch rise of a stair it puts us at a perfect height for kissing. Yes, I pay my tolls in kisses with my darling wife—when going down a stairway I always walk one step in front of Joy and will turn without notice and say, "Toll!" She returns the favor when we are walking up stairs. We both enjoy catching each other off guard, and collecting kisses in payment.

There are expensive tolls, which require long passionate kisses in payment, and small inexpensive tolls that simply call for a quick peck on the cheek. Sometimes the tolls repeat for each step on a stairway; it can take us a long time to get up just one flight. I proposed to Joy at the Washington Monument; the stairway there has 555 steps. These days everyone has to use the elevator. Can you imagine the stairwell traffic jams if they didn't?

Escalators are great for expensive tolls (long kisses) but you must be careful not to fall when nearing the end of your ride. In our area the subway system has escalators that are hundreds of feet long. It can be breathtaking!

⁓

Start collecting kissing tolls from your partner.

They will be glad to pay!

Picture This!

Kevin

~

JOY AND I HAD BEEN DATING for a while when she commented on the fact that she didn't have any nice pictures of me for her desk. Pictures weren't a big thing for me, so I didn't think much of it.

Then one day, I was walking through the mall and noticed a shop that creates glamorous photos. It was just before Christmas and I thought, "What the heck? I'll give it a try." I walked in and scheduled an appointment. I got sixteen poses, head and shoulder shots, with as many different looks and outfits as I wanted for the photos. While they had numerous costumes for women, as a man, I would have to bring my own.

I chose to have four series of four shots done. First in a coat and tie, then in my burgundy sweater—Joy's favorite! Next, with a black leather jacket over the sweater, and finally the "bad boy" look with a black T-shirt under the leather jacket. The photographer was great about getting different expressions from me to make each picture just a little bit different.

Sitting in the glass enclosed storefront waiting room with ten women waiting to get their pictures taken didn't make me feel like much of a He-Man. But the real surprise came when I found out I had to wear makeup! "Just a little powder to even out the complexion," the makeup artist assured me. I consoled myself with the thought that even Arnold has to wear makeup when he shoots *The Terminator* movies.

The photographer showed me the results on a video screen and I had to choose the ones I wanted. They turned out great!

I chose two for Joy, one for her desk and one for home. I also bought picture frames.

Joy loved the photos. Her friends at work all had pictures of their sweethearts, and she wanted one too. The "bad boy" shot was a big hit also. Those photos sure put her in a romantic frame of mind!

～

Give a romantic gift of yourself—in a photograph!

Dining Adventures

Kevin

~

YOU'LL FIND IN MOST metropolitan areas that local magazines and newspapers print guides to dining. In our area a local magazine puts out a yearly list of the "100 Very Best Restaurants" in the region. They also have a list called "Cheap Eats" which is defined as a meal for two people for $50 or less. We have friends that make a game of trying to get to all the restaurants within the year.

Joy and I have our own list. We pick and choose from the magazine lists and add to it with the recommendations of friends and family. One of the goals of our list is to experience as many different cuisines, and cultures, as possible. We've eaten meals in restaurants featuring Cajun, Caribbean, French, German, Persian, and Peruvian foods. Each time we visit a new ethnic restaurant we try to learn a little bit about that culture. It's amazing how much better the service can be if you know a little something about the waiter's country.

~

Add spice and culture to your dining by making your own romantic restaurant list. Select ten different restaurants for dinner dates by the end of the year and post it next to your calendar. Vary the cuisine and the price range so that you can dress up for an elegant date or go casual for a comfortable and relaxing evening. Let's eat!

Lots of Ways
to Say I Love You

Kevin

~

JOY AND I WERE WALKING along one afternoon when I looked over
and said *Ich Leibe Dich*. I explained that I'd said "I love you" in
German. She laughed and replied *Eu te amo*, which is "I love you"
in Portuguese. It quickly became a game and we continued until
we'd come up with fourteen different ways to say "I love you." It
was fun, educational, and romantic. Joy was raised in Brazil and
speaks fluent Portuguese, so I use *Eu te amo* quite a bit. She
appreciates it every time. Learn to say "I love you" in lots of languages and declare your love in a different way every day.

Ek het jou lief	Afrikaans
Te dua	Albanian
Bahebbek	Arabic to the female
Bahebbak	Arabic to the male
Amit tomakay bala basi	Bangla
Ami Tomake Bhalobashi	Bengali (Eastern India)
Volim te	Bosnian
obitcham te	Bulgarian
Oun Saleng Bon	Cambodian—girl to guy
Bon Saleng Oun	Cambodian—guy to girl
Ngo oi ney	Cantonese
Nali ku temwa	Chibemba (Zambia)
Volim te	Croatian

Miluji Te	Czech
Jeg elsker dig	Danish
Ik hou van jou	Dutch
I love you	English
afekereshe alhu	Ethiopian
Mahal Kita	Filipino
Iniibig Kita	Filipino
Minä rakastan sinua	Finnish
'k'ou van ui	Flemmish of the part of Ghent
Je t'aime	French
Ich liebe Dich	German
S'agapo	Greek
agapo se	Greek
oo tane prem karu chu	Gujarati
Ina sonki	Hausa (Nigeria)
Aloha au ia'oe	Hawaiian
Ani ohav etkhen	Hebrew feminine plural
Ani ohav otakh	Hebrew feminine singular
Ani ohav etkhem	Hebrew masculine or mixed plural
Ani ohaw otkha	Hebrew masculine singular
Main Tumse Pyaar Karta Hun	Hindi
Szeretlek	Hungarian
Ég elska þig	Icelandic
Ay-ayaten ka	Ilokano (Phillipines)
Aku Cinta Kamu	Indonesian
Ti amo/Ti voglio bene	Italian
Sukiyo	Japanese
Achamin	Kalenjin (Kenya)

Ninakupenda	Kiswahili (Kenya)
Sarang Ham-nida	Korean
Te Amo	Latin
Bahibak	Lebanese
Myliu tave	Lithuanian
Ech hun dech gären	Luxembourgish
Te Sakam	Macedonian
Jas Te Sakam	Macedonian
Saya kasih awak	Malay
Inhobbok	Maltese
Wo ai ni	Mandarin
jeg elsker deg	Norwegian
I ovelay ouyay	Pig Latin
Kocham cie	Polish
Eu te amo	Portuguese
Te iubesc	Romanian
Ya tyebya lyublyu	Russian
Mon rahkistan tonu	Saame, Lappish, the north of Finland
Hajem te	Sanjak
'S tough leam ort	Scottish Gaelic
Volim te	Serbian (accent 'O')
Lubim ta	Slovak
Ljubim te	Slovenian
Ke o Rata	South Sotho
Yo te amo	Spanish
te quiero	Spanish
Mame adhare	Srilanka
Jag älskar dig	Swedish

Mahal kita	Tagalog
Ninnu Nenu Premesthunanu	Telugu (south part of India)
chun luk ter	Thai
Khao raak thoe	Thai (affectionate, sweet, loving)
Seni seviyorum	Turkish
May tum say pyar karta hun	Urdu (Pakistan)
Em yeu Anh	Vietnamese—female
Anh yeu Em	Vietnamese—male
Rwy'n dy garu di	Welsh
Mo fe ran re	Yoruba (Nigeria)
Ndinokuda	Zimbabwe
Mina funani wena	Zulu

Disclaimer: We are not language experts, and we do not guarantee the accuracy of the above information. Many languages have more than one way to express love. Since there are more than 6,000 languages in the world, we know ours is not a comprehensive list.

Surreptitious Surprises

Kevin

~

IT'S A TOSS-UP IN MY MIND whether surprise or anticipation creates the biggest impact when doing something for your partner. The ideas in this section definitely fit on the surprise side of the ledger.

Romantic cards or notes delivered unexpectedly create a feeling of warmth, cheerfulness, and being cared about. There are a number of ways in which to surprise someone with a card or note.

- Slip a card into her planner notebook—as she checks her schedule the brightly colored card will fall out, bringing a surprise to her day.
- Mail cards to her office. (This makes her the envy of her coworkers.)
- Leave a card on the computer keyboard.
- Send an e-mail card.
- Leave a card under her windshield wiper (make sure to put it in a plastic zipper bag if you leave it overnight; this will keep the dew from ruining it).

~

With just a little thought, you can come up with your own unique ways of surprising your partner.

Dance Lessons

Kevin

～

EVER WATCH those old Fred and Ginger movies and wish you could dance like that? While you and your partner may not be able to duplicate their fancy moves, you can still learn to do a flashy dip or a graceful spin. Take dance lessons!

Joy and I signed up to take a series of eight classes together. We learned to foxtrot, waltz, tango, cha-cha, and swing. For those not into ballroom dancing there's Cajun and Zydeco dancing, country two-step, line dancing, Celtic dancing, and swing. There's also round dance, square dance, samba, and lambada. The health conscious can even take aerobic dance together!

～

If you feel awkward, don't let that stop you; almost everyone has some sense of rhythm. It's not hard to learn a few steps, and it's fun to do together.

Sign up for some dance lessons now!

Surprise Ending

Kevin

~

JOY'S BOSS REWARDED HER with an offer to buy a special dinner. Joy had heard of a place in Annapolis, Maryland, that was rated as one of the 100 best restaurants in the United States. It's called Treaty of Paris. We planned for an early dinner on a Saturday night. Unbeknownst to Joy, I had surprise plans for our trip to Annapolis. In addition to our special dinner, I booked us for a night at one of Annapolis' five historic inns.

The afternoon of our trip I told Joy that I needed to pick something up at the mall. While we were there I just "happened" to see a summer outfit for Joy in a window. I suggested that she try it on. I told her it was beautiful on her and bought it for her.

That night we had a wonderful dinner in a candlelit room. The food was excellent, and the company better. After dessert I suggested we do a walking tour of the city to work off the meal. I carefully lead Joy to the historic district and to the inn. I remarked that it looked interesting and suggested we visit.

Inside was decorated in antique furniture and classic fabrics, and I asked Joy if she'd like to check out our room. Suddenly it all came together for her. It was a very romantic evening made special by Joy's plans and my surprise ending to the evening.

~

Make up your own surprise ending to an
evening with your mate!

Musical Picnic

Kevin

~

JOY AND I ARE LUCKY in many things; just one is where we live. During the spring and summer there are free outdoor concerts featuring a variety of performers. These performances are sponsored by radio stations, by the city, or county. The military also has some excellent groups. One of my favorites is the Air Force jazz band—Airmen of Note.

It was a sunny Friday evening, still plenty of daylight left to enjoy after a long work week. Joy had packed a picnic basket full of goodies. Couples and families were spread all over the lawn on blankets and kites flew high overhead. The brass on the band's uniforms sparkled, and the rich music, mixed with the summer breeze, wafted over us. It was a very relaxing way to ease into the weekend. We even got to enjoy the sunset on our drive home.

~

Most city newspapers have a listing of
upcoming cultural events. Find out where outdoor
concerts are listed in your city, get a copy of the
coming events, and make a date!

Our Engagement Story

Joy

~

IT WAS A TYPICAL MONDAY afternoon at work. I was catching up on some paperwork late in the afternoon when I got a phone call from Kevin. He asked me to come down to the lobby to meet him. I was confused.

What was Kevin doing at my office building in the middle of a workday? What a pleasant surprise to have him drop by.

I hastened to the elevators and in a few minutes was greeted with a smile, a hug, and a kiss. I'm sure the question showed on my face, but Kevin just said, "Come with me." He started for the door.

I hesitated, since I hadn't told my boss I was leaving and my purse was still at my desk. Kevin just smiled and propelled me out the door.

By that time I figured I had better stop asking questions. Instead I took a deep breath, relaxed, and prepared for whatever romantic adventure Kevin had in store. I had no idea what was coming.

We got in his car and drove towards downtown Washington D.C. It was a lovely spring day and I enjoyed watching the scenery. Soon we were near my favorite D.C. landmark, the Washington Monument. It certainly stands out as the tallest building for miles, and I've always enjoyed gazing up at it.

To my surprise and delight, we parked and walked up the grassy slope towards the obelisk. The line of people waiting to go up to the top of the Monument often wraps around the base two or three times. We were in luck! We could see the end of the line only half way around, and we hurried to join it.

Alas! When we did get there, we encountered a Park Service ranger who informed us that the Monument would close at 4:30 P.M., and those already in line would be the last ones for the day. No wonder the line was so short! We looked at each other in dismay, wondering what to do next. We came all this way just to be disappointed!

Then Kevin spoke quietly to the ranger, "Can I talk to you a minute?" I stepped away a few paces to give them some privacy and looked around. I was wondering what Kevin could possibly say to the ranger that would make any difference. On the other hand, Kevin can be very persuasive. The next thing I knew, we were escorted to the Monument entrance and promptly put on the next elevator up, ahead of all the others who were waiting patiently for their turn. Hmm . . . something was up, and it wasn't just the elevator.

It takes about 90 seconds to get to the top (it's a long way up), but it seemed like no time at all. Kevin and I held hands as we stepped out onto the viewing level. There are small windows on each side, and we peered out of each one. Finally I turned to Kevin with that question still in my eyes, and waited for him to say something.

"Joy, here at the top of the Washington Monument, where we can see everyone and everyone can see us, I want to ask you to marry me." He brought out a small box that could only hold a ring. "Will you marry me?"

"Yes!"

The two Park Service rangers and their supervisor were all waiting by the doorway as we exited the elevator to leave. They wanted to know how it had turned out. They were very pleased to be the first to congratulate us on our engagement.

Creative Engagement

Shawn S., Minnesota

~

On September 1, 1990 Jennifer and I had our first date—dinner at the Signature Cafe (an Egyptian restaurant), and a walk through Prospect Park. We spent a couple of hours in the park after dinner talking about life and each other, and getting a better idea of who we were, and we saw a beautiful sunset together.

After a year of dating we agreed that keeping our romance alive while we were both away at college would be too difficult. We kept in contact, and dated, on and off, over the next seven years. On Valentine's Day in 1997 we got back together again.

On September 1, 1999 I invited Jennifer out for dinner. We arrived at the Signature Cafe around 7:00 P.M. and found that the restaurant was closed. I knew this already, but I pretended to be very disappointed and told her we would find somewhere else to eat. As we left the little residential neighborhood we passed Prospect Park. I asked her to go for a walk.

As we climbed the steps to the top of the hill, she saw my sister with a video camera recording our arrival. She also saw a candlelit table set for two. Playing from a boom box nearby was Egyptian music.

By this point she had put all the pieces together and looked rather pale. I thought some food might help that, and served up some bobaganoush and chicken with rice. She seemed a bit confused as she repeated over and over again, "What are you doing, Shawn?" and "We haven't even talked about this." I told her it was just a nice dinner, and that we should enjoy the food. We finished dinner in silence, and I asked her to open her card.

The front of the card had a collage of pictures of us, and a line of text wrapping around it that said, "The time I have spent with you has given me memories I will cherish forever." Inside I had written my heartfelt message and marriage proposal.

She read the card and I got down on my knee and opened a small box containing a diamond solitaire engagement ring. I slipped it on her finger and asked her "Will you marry me?" I did not get an answer; she just sat there staring at the ring.

Finally, I cleaned up the table and we walked quietly down to the car and put everything away. We then went for a walk and ended up back on top of the hill admiring the same view we shared on that bench nine years before. As we sat quietly she murmured a few words, "You never asked me." Apparently she had been in shock, and didn't even hear me the first time I asked her! I got down on my knees and asked her again. The response was "No, ask me like in the card." So I began reciting from memory all I could remember in the card. She finally said, "It would be my incredible honor."

~

A proposal is an extraordinary event in the lives of two people. When you are ready to propose, take the time to make it special, unique, and unforgettable. Think about the memorable moments in your relationship, the interests you share, etc. Use these ideas as a starting point to personalize your proposal. Be creative. Here are some possible proposal settings to get you started.

- *on a boat*
- *via videotape*
- *under the stars*
- *on a golf course*
- *in a Chinese restaurant (think fortune cookie)*
- *out of a magician's hat*
- *in the newspaper*
- *on a rented billboard*
- *on a ski lift*
- *at church*
- *in a hot air balloon*
- *at the gym*
- *on a roller coaster*
- *at the beach*
- *in cyberspace*

*Come up with a plan, enlist the support
and participation of family and friends if needed,
take a deep breath, and go for it!*

Kevin

Grand Canyon

Kevin

ONE OF THE THINGS that has always impressed me about Joy is her adventuresome spirit. When she mentioned she wanted to raft the Grand Canyon, I impulsively said, "Let's do it!" Floating down a lazy river on a raft seemed a wonderfully romantic thing to do. Only later did Joy mention the Colorado River rapids.

We booked a twelve-day trip with an experienced outfitter. Over the course of the next year we planned and talked and shopped for the trip. Finally we were on our way. In Flagstaff, AZ, we transferred clothes, sleeping bags, and tents into rubber trip bags to keep everything dry. Then we all loaded onto a bus for the trip to Lee's Ferry to begin our adventure. Once we were on the river, it didn't take long for us to reach the first rapids. Woohoo! And that was only the beginning! Over the next twelve days we traveled over 200 miles of river and went over what seemed like 100 rapids. Our guides shared their extensive knowledge of the geography and history of the canyon as we went along.

One of the things I most enjoyed was sharing the beauty of the canyon with Joy. It was fun to wake up every morning with the sun just peeking over the rim of the cliffs surrounding us, to soak in the quiet around us, away from civilization and cell phones. As we made our way down the river there was always something new to see around the bend: water, rocks, light, and perspective. The trip gave me a new appreciation for life and God's handiwork.

The most perilous part of our journey turned out to be not on water but on land. Around mile 157 Havasu Creek enters the river and we stopped to hike up the creek to Havasu Falls. As we stepped down some rock ledges, Joy and I lost our balance and fell about eight feet. Ouch! I was hobbling around for two days, and Joy got a whopper of a bruise. Fortunately, that was the extent of our injuries.

Near the end of the trip is Lava Falls, the most dangerous rapid, which drops over thirty feet in two stages. I heard the roar of the rapid from far upstream; the excitement built as the noise steadily increased. We stopped to scout the rapid before running it. Our raft made it through okay, but one of the others flipped. By this time we were experienced at pulling people out of the water and everyone was rescued quickly. Before we knew it, we were sitting in a restaurant in Flagstaff celebrating our success with all the rafters and guides.

During the trip Joy and I learned a lot about each other and how we deal with life. It made me love her even more.

If you are an adventurous romantic couple, consider adventure travel for your next vacation. In choosing a trip, think about your budget, interests, time frame, and endurance. You can push yourselves to the limit skiing to the North Pole, enjoy biking together past Italian vineyards, or snuggle in a tent after hiking in Grand Teton National Park.

If you don't have time for a trip, look around your local area for day-trip possibilities, such as:

- Hiking trails
- Whitewater rafting
- Horseback riding
- Kayaking
- Spelunking
- Rock climbing

Check the Appendix for more adventure travel resources.

Personalized Romance Novel

Kevin

~

Love's Next Door—chapter nine excerpt:

"Kevin, I really enjoyed myself this afternoon. Would you care to come in for a bite to eat?" Joy asked, as she unlocked the front door to her home.

Kevin stood watching as the fading sunlight caught the ends of her blonde hair, turning them a golden hue. The whole time they were together, the feelings that had been hidden for so long suddenly came rushing back to life. Every turn of her head, brush of her arm, and sound of her laughter, made him want to hold her and smother her with kisses. And those breathtaking blue eyes!

"Hello, Kevin! Are you there?"

His face suddenly flushed, making Joy laugh. "Sure, I'd love to come in. I thought you'd never ask," he said, smiling broadly, climbing the steps and entering into the foyer.

Joy took his coat and hung it next to hers.

Love's Next Door is a personalized romance novel from Books by You Publishing, and this excerpt is a preview from their Web site. I hate to make generalizations, but I believe, and the statistics bear out, that most women love romance novels. The twist is that instead of reading about someone else, personalization allows you and your mate to be the leading characters, with more than thirty characteristics you can customize.

There are a number of Web sites for personalized romance novels you can find on the Web. All seem to be priced between $30–$50. You can find three different romances at *www.bookbyyou.com,* or get one of the many story lines available in "wild" or "mild" versions at *www.yournovel.com.* Another story option can be found at *www.paradiseworks-inc.com* where your novel is set in the romantic Hawaiian Islands.

The wide smile on Joy's face told me that ordering her starring role in a romance novel was the right thing to do. She's excited about her book and can't wait to see the finished work. She's sure her friends will be impressed and probably a little jealous, too.

≈

Order a personalized romance novel

for your partner. You'll both spend hours

of time reading it again and again.

Touch

Joy

~

KEVIN AND I HAD SURVIVED our first day of whitewater rafting through the Grand Canyon. After dinner we retired to our tent on the sandy bank of the Colorado River. We were proud of ourselves, exhausted, and bone weary from the trip. I gently took one of Kevin's feet in my hands and began massaging away the aches of the day. Kevin sighed deeply. It was quiet except for the river sounds. The massage was for myself as much as for Kevin—a way to connect with each other after a long day.

You may not be able to get away to the Grand Canyon, but the power of touch is available to you wherever you are. I often come up behind Kevin as he is sitting at the computer and massage his neck and shoulders, just as a way to say "Hi, I love you."

It's important to touch the people we love. Many studies have been done on the benefits of touch. People of all ages respond to massage. It can give us a greater sense of love, warmth, and security.

~

Give your partner a loving massage to rub away

their worries. It's a wonderful way to begin

or end a romantic evening.

Romantic Turnoff

Kevin

~

IN LATE APRIL there is a National TV-Turnoff Week. Turning off the TV will give you an amazing amount of free time to be romantic. Try it today and make use of these seven quick ideas for what to do instead.

1. **Dinner and dancing.** Make reservations at your favorite restaurant and then spend the rest of the evening dancing the night away. At a club, or at home, swaying sensually to the rhythm of the music is very romantic.

2. **Cook dinner together.** Don't forget the romantic music and candles. Afterward, spend some time together creating a personal cookbook of your favorite recipes.

3. **Visit the library.** Visit the section on poetry, check out a book, and spend the evening reading to each other.

4. **Go for a walk.** Weather permitting, there aren't many things more romantic than walking hand in hand.

5. **Talk to each other.** Joy and I like to use a pattern we learned in our communications class. Share something you appreciate about your mate. Let him or her know of any new information about your plans for the day and immediate future. Question them about anything that has been puzzling you lately. Deliver a complaint only if you can follow it with a request for change to alleviate the situation (your mate has the right to accept or refuse your request). Finally share your wishes, hopes, and dreams.

6. **Spend the evening writing love letters to each other**. Seal the letters in the envelopes, walk down to the mailbox together, and drop them in the mail. They'll be a pleasant reminder later in the week about the love of your mate.

7. **Clip it.** Stop by the store on the way home and pick up a few magazines. Pick a variety of subjects that interest both of you. When you get home spend time reading the magazines and clip a few articles from each for discussion. Talk with your partner about what interested you and why.

~

These tips make it easy to spend a week with your mate away from the TV. Enjoy!

Browsing the Bookshelves

Joy

~

ONE THING THAT DISTINGUISHES the area in which we live is the number of antiquarian bookstores. There are almost forty used bookshops. They present great opportunities to be romantic! Kevin and I love to browse the stacks of old books. We've even created games for it:

- Select a section and see how many books you can find with the words love or romance in the title (really difficult if you get stuck with the archeology section).
- Find the shortest, longest, worst, or best love poem among the poetry books. Reading it aloud is mandatory.
- Find the oldest book on love or marriage. What are the best and worst ideas inside?

Many used bookstores are housed in rambling old homes, with various rooms, hallways, and nooks and crannies filled with books. Nooks and crannies also provide excellent places to steal kisses!

We usually leave with at least one or two books and at $1 or $2 a trip, it's a fun yet inexpensive date. You can also try this at your local library.

~

Spend an evening browsing
the bookshelves to find romance.

Putt-Putt

Kevin

~

I MADE PLANS FOR A SATURDAY afternoon to surprise Joy. I just told her to dress for a spring afternoon. The weather was perfect for outdoor activities.

When the appointed time came I handed Joy a golf ball on which I'd drawn a big red heart. Joy had a puzzled look on her face. "We're going golfing?" Joy and I can be competitive, but the difference in our sizes can give me an unfair advantage in some sports (Joy is 5'1" and I'm 6'1"). "Golf with a twist," I replied, and off we went to play miniature golf (also known as putt-putt).

Putt-Putt is a great opportunity for us to compete without taking ourselves too seriously, enjoy the weather, and also be romantic. We gamble on our putt-putt, for kisses. And a hole-in-one gets a bonus kiss. Sometimes I'll even carry a few Hershey's kisses in my pocket for a change of pace.

Our favorite courses are the silliest ones, with loops, terraces, and goofy obstacles. That way when we do miss we can blame it on the course, laugh it off, and still have fun.

~

Get competitive and gamble on the golf course!
A putt-putt course, that is, and don't forget
the bonus kisses.

We Volunteer

Kevin

~

IT DIDN'T APPEAR to be the most romantic date when Joy invited me to join her as a volunteer to serve meals to the homeless. It seemed like an interesting and worthwhile project though and I was glad to help. Four other volunteers joined Joy and me in the dining hall and set to work preparing the meal. The quantities seemed huge but we had a lot of people to feed.

As our guests arrived Joy and I began preparing plates of food and drinks. We served dozens of people over the next two hours, playfully bumping into each other in the small kitchen as we kept hot food flowing.

By the time the doors closed we were exhausted but we still had work to do. We all pitched in and cleaned up, scrubbing pots and floors, and leaving the kitchen and dining room ready for the next crew.

When we signed up as volunteers, we didn't really know what we were getting into. What we got was a feeling of accomplishment, the knowledge that we are truly blessed, and a renewed love and appreciation for each other.

There are so many ways you can volunteer to help out your community:

- read stories to children
- deliver meals to shut-ins
- tutor in computer skills
- staff a charity walk
- teach English as a Second Language

- play with kids
- give blood
- help build a house
- clean up a nature trail

There are many local organizations that match volunteer opportunities to your schedule and interests.

∼

Volunteer together with your partner.

It's a uniquely romantic way to share with

each other as well as with others.

Anchors Aweigh!

Joy

~

KEVIN AND I recently participated in the following exercise:
Compare your mate to these nautical vessels, and choose the one that best describes him or her. When each of you is ready, take turns explaining why you chose that particular vessel. Then have your partner tell you what vessel they would have picked for themselves.

Tenacious Tug Boat
Toy Sail Boat
Tom Sawyer Wood Raft
Cruising Yacht
High-Speed Motorboat
Venetian Gondola
Mythical Treasure Ship
Sleek Hydrofoil
Mississippi River Ferry Boat
Rubber Dinghy
Old-Fashioned Row Boat
Clipper Ship

The choices were difficult. I closed my eyes and tried to imagine myself as a boat. I finally settled on "Old Fashioned Row Boat" because I consider myself practical, not fancy, and I try to take time to enjoy the scenery along the way.

Kevin, however, had other ideas. He told me he couldn't choose just one. He said I was romantic like a Venetian Gondola, adventurous like Tom Sawyer on his Wood Raft, and beautiful like a Sleek Hydrofoil. I was absolutely bowled over by his words. Did he really think of me in those glowing images, when my vision of myself was so limited? He viewed me through the eyes of love and I liked what he saw.

Share this exercise with your "First Mate" today!

~

More information on this exercise can be found in Beginnings *by Lyman Coleman (Serendipity House, Inc., 1987).*

Top Ten Romantic Songs

Kevin

~

JOY AND I have very eclectic tastes in music. There are literally hundreds of romantic songs we enjoy listening to together. We compiled a list of our top ten romantic music picks for you. Just like our list of top ten movies this list keeps growing; it's now up to twenty-five.

1. *Grow Old with Me*, John Lennon
2. *My Cherie Amour*, Stevie Wonder
3. *Cherish*, The Association
4. *Someone to Watch over Me*, Willie Nelson
5. *Take My Eyes Off of You*, Franki Valli
6. *More Than You Know*, Perry Como
7. *Can't Help Falling in Love*, Elvis Presley
8. *Unforgettable*, original by Nat King Cole and the rerecorded duet with Natalie Cole
9. *As Time Goes By*, Dooley Wilson
10. *When I Fall in Love*, Celine Dion and Clive Griffin
11. *Keeper of the Stars*, Tracy Byrd
12. *The Wonder of You*, Elvis Presley
13. *Love Me Tender*, Elvis Presley
14. *A Natural Woman*, Carole King
15. *Moon River*, Andy Williams
16. *We've Only Just Begun*, The Carpenters

17. *Three Times a Lady*, The Commodores
18. *The Color of My Love*, Celine Dion
19. *Just the Way You Are*, Billy Joel
20. *More Than Words*, Extreme
21. *My Girl*, Temptations
22. *Shower the People*, James Taylor
23. *Every Breath You Take*, The Police
24. *Unchained Melody*, Roy Orbison
25. *Something*, The Beatles

Once you have your list, make a songbook. I like to occasionally sing to Joy, so I've created a romance songbook to help me remember the lyrics. Nothing fancy, just printed pages in a notebook, but she really likes it when I pull it out.

You can also make a cassette tape or burn a CD of your romantic favorites. This is a very personal, thoughtful, and inexpensive gift. Joy recorded a tape for me once, which included romantic messages between the songs. I played it so often that the tape wore out!

~

Make a list of your favorite songs with your sweetheart

today! You can use your list to be romantic.

Part Four

Married

"The Passionate Shepherd to His Love"

Come live with me, and be my love,
And we will all the pleasures prove
That valleys, groves, hills and fields,
Woods, or sleepy mountain yields.

And we will sit upon the rocks
Seeing the shepherds feed their flocks,
By shallow rivers to whose falls
Melodious birds sing madrigals

And I will make thee beds of roses
And a thousand fragrant posies,
A cap of flowers, and a kirtle
Embroidered all the leaves of myrtle;

A gown made of the finest wool
Which from our pretty lambs we pull;
Fair lines slippers for the cold,
With buckles of the purest gold;

A belt of straw and ivy-buds,
With coral clasps and amber studs;
And if these pleasures may thee move,
Come live with me, and be my love.

The shepherds' swains shall dance and sing
For thy delight each May morning:
If these delights thy mind may move,
Then live with me, and be my love.

Christopher Marlowe

Our Wedding Story

Kevin

~

A WEDDING IS A SPECIAL DAY for every bride and groom, and ours was no exception. Singing a duet with my bride as part of the ceremony will always be a highlight for me. Many of our guests played parts in our wedding. We treasure their friendship and the love they showed for us.

The night before the wedding, we rehearsed the ceremony at our chosen site—a gazebo in a public park. It was a beautiful fall evening. After the rehearsal we walked a block to a nearby church for the rehearsal dinner. After dinner we put the families to work creating arrangements for the ceremony and reception from the bunches of flowers we had purchased. The one rule we had was that no arrangement could be completed without participation from both families. They did a marvelous job. It was a great way for them to meet and get to know each other before the wedding.

The next morning I woke up to the sound of rain on the roof. "Oh no, there goes our outdoor wedding!" Serendipitously, the minister of the church where we had the rehearsal dinner called us and offered to let us use the church for the ceremony. It all worked out better than I could have hoped, and the service was beautiful.

Having our friends and family involved not only made our wedding more meaningful, but it also reduced our costs dramatically!

The following tips will help you have a romantic wedding on a small budget.

- Use your network of friends to assist you; ours were an amazing amount of help to us—Barbara designed and printed the invitations and thank you cards; Mary Lou did the planning; Tom did the cake; Randy did the catering; Felicia played piano for the prelude and recessional; Tim and Dennis ushered; Carol played the flute for the processional; Kendrea gave the opening prayer; Jim performed the ceremony; Keith, Ruth, Sandra, Simone, Susan W., Sylvia, Don, Lynne, Diane, Brad, and Susan B. all sang during the service.
- Borrow what you can—linens, baskets, or flowers from your neighbor's garden—we borrowed a party tent to use for cover which really helped with the light rain we had during the reception.
- Use a free or low-cost site for the wedding and reception—our original site was a park gazebo and although we ended up in a nearby church the cost was minimal (stay away from the country clubs and hotels that not only are expensive but also require you to use their catering services).
- Make your own—decorations, favors, and headpieces—we made our own flower arrangements, which was fun and saved money.

∽

We hope our tips and ideas help you
to have a wonderful, memorable,
and romantic wedding. Ours sure was!

Priority

Kevin

~

THERE ARE 164 HOURS IN A WEEK. How do you spend those hours? What are your priorities? When does romance fit into your schedule? What priority do you give your partner?

The average person sleeps about seven hours a night, meaning that sleep takes up forty-nine of your 164 hours, leaving 115.

The average person spends an average of four hours a day on meals (shopping, preparing, eating, and cleaning up after). Subtract another twenty-eight of the 115 hours leaving eighty-seven hours.

Work or school, along with getting ready, and commuting to and from, takes an average of fifty hours a week. You have thirty-seven hours left.

Household chores take another eight hours a week. This leaves you with twenty-nine hours.

We're sure that you can think of many more things that take up your time. But where are your priorities? What do you value most? Joy and I place a high value on our relationship. We spend at least an hour each week talking with each other about romance and our relationship. It really helps us get past small talk about everyday things and helps us focus on us.

~

Make your relationship a priority and allocate time to spend with your mate. Take a hard look at where you spend your time and what your priorities are. Try to allocate at least one hour a week to spend on romance. You'll be very glad you did.

Doing the Dishes

Kevin

~

WHILE DOING THE DISHES certainly doesn't seem romantic, Joy and I have borrowed an idea from her aunt and uncle that helps us keep in touch and can certainly set the tone for a romantic evening.

We take turns reading to each other while the other person cleans up the kitchen and does the dishes. It makes what could be an onerous task much more enjoyable. "Sharing" the task like this lightens the load for me. The time passes quickly and we both feel connected to each other. The reading can also be a springboard to interesting discussions on a variety of topics.

Any type of reading materials will do—choose your favorite topic and read away! It almost made me look forward to doing dishes!

~

The next time you have an ordinary dinner at home,

start the romance with an after-dinner read.

A Sticky Situation

Kevin and Joy

~

THANK GOODNESS for the scientist at 3M whose scrap paper bookmarks kept falling out of his church choir hymnal. Scientist Art Fry had seen a demonstration of a new adhesive created by a coworker and realized it could be used for a convenient and reliable bookmark. Post-it Notes are the result and they help me be romantic. The notes come in many colors and sizes, which are great for leaving romantic notes everywhere. There are even heart-shaped Post-it Notes available.

We leave them in books, in cabinets, the medicine chest, in dresser drawers, on windows, in CD cases, on mirrors, on doors, and even in the refrigerator. Some of the best reactions come from notes hidden in unusual places. The look on Joy's face when she saw one in the breadmaker was great, and when Kevin lifted the toilet lid and found a love note stuck to the bottom was he ever surprised!

Here are some ideas for places to put sticky notes:

- in pockets in clothing
- in his lunchbox or bag
- hidden in the bath towels
- on the bed
- stuck in the current book she's reading
- on videotape cases
- rolled up in socks
- stuck in shoes
- sticking out of magazines

- inside CD cases
- on or inside food packages
- on the inside of the lid on the can of Folgers coffee with this note "Forget the coffee, *You* are the best part of my morning!"
- on the alarm clock—he or she feels loved right from the start of the day

～

Get yourself some sticky notes,

and be sticky sweet with your mate!

Gift Basket

Joy

~

KEVIN WAS PLANNING a business trip out of town for a conference. I knew he was going to be very busy with meetings around the clock, and I wanted to let him know that I was thinking of him. Meals were provided for the conference attendees, so I knew he wasn't going to starve. Still, he was trying to maintain a healthy diet, which is sometimes difficult when you don't have menu choices.

I decided to have a fruit basket delivered to his hotel room. That way he would have healthy snacks whenever he wanted, as well as a reminder that I loved him. I called a local delivery service to place my order, and I checked with the hotel desk to make sure they would get the basket to Kevin.

Kevin left the next morning. That night I waited by the phone to hear his reaction to my surprise. He loved it, of course, and I was glad to hear his voice and picture his smile. He described the basket in great detail and told me it was beautifully done up with bows and cellophane. The fruit looked delicious and was perfectly ripe. He really enjoyed having access to healthy snacks while he was there. When he got back he told me the fruit was sweet, just like me.

Gift baskets are a welcome change to the usual candy and flowers. Most florists will deliver fruit baskets on request, and there are a number of specialty delivery services as well. Gift baskets can include almost anything, and often have a central theme. You can order one or make your own. The following are some suggestions.

- **Pamper Her**—relaxing fragrances, bubble bath, body lotion, a bath net, scented candles, and potpourri
- **Movie Night**—your favorite romantic video, microwave popcorn, sodas, chocolate chip cookies, and red licorice
- **Picnic in the Park**—two wineglasses, sparkling cider, two cloth napkins, Brie, crackers, and shortbread cookies

A gift basket says you love and care in more ways than one. Give your sweetheart a basket full of love!

Dream Posters

Kevin

~

JOY AND I EACH DID THE FOLLOWING EXERCISE about "I wish I had's." While the exercise is intended primarily to help you focus where your time is spent, we found it very useful in finding out about each other's wishes and dreams.

This exercise is taken from *Taking Control of Your Time and Your Life* by Dick Lohr.

Start with a pad of paper and a pencil. At the top of the paper write "Today I am ninety-five." Now picture yourself at age ninety-five. Your family has just thrown a ninety-fifth birthday shindig for you. You have just eaten your single cupcake with a single candle on top. After the party you retreat to the front porch to sit in your rocker. You put a sweater around your shoulders to keep off the night air. You begin thinking about your life. For the most part you feel satisfied, but as you look down at your feet you find a basket filled with slips of paper. On each slip of paper is a statement beginning with the words "I wish I had ____." What do they say?

Take ten minutes to jot down all the "I wish I had's" you would find in your basket. Here are a few of mine.

I wish I had . . .

- learned to paint
- traveled to the South Seas
- learned to dance
- spent more time with my partner
- taken a cruise through the Panama Canal

- flown on the Concorde
- visited Tibet
- planted a flower garden
- sung in a choir

When we were done brainstorming, we gathered up some old magazines and cut out pictures that represented items on our wish lists. We pasted them to some posterboard to create special Dream Posters. Joy had them framed and they're on the wall in our computer room to remind us. Joy's has a cruise ship, hot air balloon, laptop computer, fireplace, massage, golf resort, and lots of beautiful flowers. Mine has a walk on the beach, a picture of the rain forest in Panama, golf, a muffaletta sandwich and beignets from New Orleans, a Dodge Spider sports car, and the Concorde because that's how I want to fly to Europe when I visit.

Be more romantic, share your dreams,
and live them together.

"Today I am ninety-five" excerpted from *Taking Control of Your Time and Your Life* by Dick Lohr, copyright © 1995 by CareerTrack publications. Reprinted by permission.

Dinner at Eight

Kevin

~

I ALWAYS KEEP A SUPPLY of humorous romance cards in my briefcase and send them to Joy when she least expects it. For this particular occasion I sent her one that included an invitation for dinner. I made sure Joy would be out for the afternoon so I could prepare. This romantic dinner was a lot of work—that didn't include cooking, because I stopped by a local gourmet store and got takeout.

First, I set the table with our wedding china. I arranged a large bouquet of flowers in a vase to use for a centerpiece. Then I got out the linen napkins with napkin rings and set out the crystal goblets. Then I set out the silverware, checking my *Miss Manners* book to make sure I got it right. I even wrote out little place cards for us. Tall fluted candles completed the table setting.

We both dressed our best for the occasion and I wore my "New Orleans School of Cooking" apron and a towel over my arm to serve.

I tried to foresee everything we would need so that I wouldn't have to rush around while Joy waited. Attention to detail is important, and I even found the seldom-used ice bucket and tongs.

When Joy arrived I was still finishing up transferring the food to the serving dishes so she offered to help. I gave her a few simple tasks like lighting candles, pouring water, and picking out some romantic music.

It was a lovely dinner! With everything prepared we had plenty of time to relax, talk, and enjoy the meal. It was very romantic!

~

It's never too late to impress your mate with good food and good manners. Invite her to dinner!

Teddy Bears

Joy

∼

IT STARTED OUT AS JUST ANOTHER ORDINARY DAY, but I was in the mood to make it special and romantic. To set the stage before Kevin got home, I recruited some forty cute and cuddly helpers who just happened to be available. My helpers were from our joint collection of teddy bears. I pinned a romantic note to each one.

Then I scattered them all over the house. Kevin was really surprised when he walked in the door and it definitely put him in the mood for romance too!

Teddy bears are a wonderful way to say, "I love you!" They are soft, cuddly, and cute. One of the things that makes a teddy a unique gift is that each one *is* unique. You can spend a lot of time picking out the perfect bear for your sweetheart. I found the Vermont Teddy Bear company on the Web. They specialize in gift teddy bears for all occasions. Their Web site also features a free virtual teddy bear delivery service.

If you can't find just the right bear on the Web, you can design and build your own teddy bear at a local Build-a-Bear Workshop. Build-a-Bear provides all the materials and tools. You provide the imagination.

∼

Share a teddy bear hug today!

Anchored

Kevin

~

I WAS READING *Honey, I Want to Start My Own Business* by Azriela Jaffe and came upon the concept of relationship anchors. These are daily rituals that help you maintain your commitment to the relationship. Anchors are extremely important when between work, kids, etc. you can quickly be overcome by events and neglect your sweetie.

Anchors can be saying "I love you" every day, a hug and a kiss when you leave and return from work, a daily phone call, or a weekly walk together hand in hand. As I read I started to think about the anchors we use to stay in tune with each other and I compiled a short list of daily and weekly anchors that Joy and I use.

Daily

- Say "I love you"
- Kiss and hug to start and end our day
- Call to check in and say "I love you" just before the kids' naptime, and again just before I leave the office for home
- Trade e-mails with updates on our day

Weekly

- Prepare a meal together
- Watch a video or movie together after the kids are asleep
- Go to church together on Sundays

Each anchor gives us time to reconnect with each other.

Please work together to complete the following exercise from the Jaffe book. Make sure to finish it by signing as indicated.

Anchoring Rituals

Completion time: 20 minutes

Amidst these crazy times, it's important that, as a minimum, we do the following with and for each other, every day or week.

1.
2.
3.
4.
5.
6.
7.
8.
9.
10.

We commit to each other that no matter how busy we get, we will make the time for those activities that center us and sustain our relationship during difficult times.

Sign your names at the end of each sentence.

～

Don't worry if you can't come up with ten—or if you come up with more. The important thing is to get you thinking about being anchored in your relationship.

"Anchoring Rituals" from *Honey, I Want to Start My Own Business* by Azriela L. Jaffe. Copyright © 1996 by Azriela Jaffe. Reprinted by permission of HarperCollins Publishers, Inc.

Riser Advertiser

Kevin

~

JOY IS AN AVID COLLEGE BASKETBALL FAN and I got this idea while watching games with her. Often as the camera pans over the crowd you'll see little advertisements on the risers for the stairs. I laughed when I first saw it. Then I realized that it was something I could use at home to show Joy my love.

Over lunch at the office one day I made up a silly version of the old roses are red poem and printed it landscape format, putting each line on a separate sheet of paper finishing with an "I Love You." I made sure that the message was on the bottom half of the page and folded them in half.

When I got home that night I used pushpins to attach the pages to the risers, I set out the messages in the stairwell and waited at the top with a rose.

"Joy! Can you come here a minute?" I called and heard her coming up the first flight of stairs. She turned the corner to the second flight of stairs and saw the first half of the poem. "Oh," she sighed.

As she came up the second flight and stopped at the landing she saw the second half along with the additional "I love you" message. Then she saw me at the top of the stairs with the flower. I got a big hug and kiss for that little trick.

~

Use your risers to send

your own message to your loved one.

Who Done It?

Kevin

~

JOY AND I FOUND A UNIQUE WAY to host a group of friends for a fun and romantic evening. We played a game called "How to Host a Murder." Joy chose the version called "The Watersdown Affair," which is set in the English countryside. We invited a small group of friends for a dinner party and asked each to play a part in the mystery. The game comes with ready-made invitations and booklets describing each person's role with suggestions for costumes.

On the night of the party I started dinner early so I'd have time to concentrate on the game. I fixed Cornish game hens with wild rice dressing and they took forever to prepare. Fortunately Joy was a great help so I didn't miss too much of the fun.

When our guests arrived I couldn't believe the work they had put into their costumes. Everyone stayed in character throughout the evening and each added a dash of their own personality. There are four rounds of clues and conversation and we worked our way through hors d'oeuvres, dinner, and dessert between the rounds. Finally, over coffee, we each chose our suspect and then Joy read the solution. Nobody guessed right, but it was still a lot of fun!

~

Host a murder mystery and act out your own romantic parts in the affair. There are several versions available at most toy stores. We recommend that you order takeout, instead of cooking, so you can relax and enjoy the game.

How to Avoid
Being a Golf Widow

Kevin

~

"I DON'T WANT TO BE A GOLF WIDOW!" Joy told me one morning as I prepared to play a round with some friends.

I suggested we could take some lessons together. She was hesitant at first, but soon was making plans and checking schedules. We took a beginning class at a local golf park with a driving range and a par-three course. The instructor spent a lot of time breaking down the swing into manageable parts so that we all felt comfortable hitting the ball.

I had been playing for almost twenty years and never had a lesson. After a few weeks I could see improvement with more accuracy and power in my shots. Joy is athletic and she made great strides with her lessons. We even played the par-three course together. It was great fun. Joy jumped up and down laughing and yelling when she made her first par!

Playing golf together gives us a chance to connect with each other in a unique and different way. We both enjoy the game, and with the close-cropped fairways, manicured greens, and skillfully designed courses, the scenery is beautiful.

~

*Try golfing together! Whether taking a lesson or out
on the course, you'll always be inspired.*

Keeping Score

Joy

~

KEVIN AND I enjoy getting the opportunity to play golf together.

Before we started out I picked up a blank scorecard. Kevin looked at me, puzzled, because I don't usually keep score. I play golf for fun.

After we walked off the first green, I drove the cart to the next tee. When Kevin got out to hit his next tee shot I scribbled a note in the first little box to keep score for the last hole: "Great shot honey." When Kevin came back he looked at the card, laughed, and gave me a big kiss.

Then after each hole Kevin had to check the scorecard for my comment and I found something novel to write for each hole. Sometimes it related to our play on the hole, like: "Just missed the groundhog!" Sometimes it was something else that happened between shots like: "I got tickled." I had to write really small, because they don't give you much room in each box. There was enough room to write after the last hole "I love you." Kevin said it was the winning score! "Keeping score" certainly made our golf game more romantic.

~

Try "keeping score" with your sweetheart, and don't limit yourself to golf. Any game with a scorecard or pad will do. Just remember to have fun and enjoy being together—that's what romance is all about.

Picture Perfect

Joy

~

I WAS AT A FAMILY WEDDING and the talk turned to romantic gestures. My family knows that Kevin and I are always interested in romantic stories. Each person at my table was trying to top the others' stories of their greatest romantic experience. After some time my cousin Tim pulled out his wallet. He didn't say a word; he merely passed his credit card across the table.

While most people do not equate credit cards or checkbooks with romance, this credit card was the most romantic monetary instrument I have ever seen!

The background of the card was a picture of Tim and his wife on their wedding day, looking radiant. Tim said he gets *oohs* and *ahs* every time he proffers his credit card. I can see why. Every time he purchases something, Tim gets a reminder of the beautiful woman he loves. And he also has the opportunity to proudly demonstrate his love to the rest of the world.

I was very impressed, and of course asked Tim for details. His card happens to be a VISA card from FirstUSA. You can find other resources on the Web.

~

This is a great way to incorporate romance
into your everyday life!

Taxed

Kevin

~

IT WAS THE LAST WEEK to prepare our taxes and get them filed before the midnight deadline on Tuesday. Joy is the numbers person in our family and she had been working hard to get everything ready. She stacked paperwork in neat little piles stretching from one end of the dining room table to the other. I inserted a little romance into her efforts.

First I created a dummy W-2r form that showed a salary for Joy with some really big numbers in each of the blocks on the form. Then I added a note at the bottom that this W-2r (the r is for romance, of course) needed a special IRS form 5683968.

Then I created a dummy tax form with that number and included it in another pile on the table. Form 5683968 ("LoveYou" on your phone keypad) had a number of blocks that correlated with the dummy W-2r. In the explanation for each block, I put stuff like "Please enter the number of kisses you received in 1999 from block 1" on the W-2r. As she filled in the form, the numbers fit into a complicated formula to determine the amount of taxes due. Funny thing about it is the amount to pay always comes out to zero.

~

Joy laughed and laughed when she saw this
and worked it out. It made a taxing situation
for her a romantic time for both of us!

Bubble Bath Break

Kevin

~

BUBBLE BATHS ARE A GOOD WAY for Joy to take a break after a really hectic day. To help you get started with giving your mate a relaxing bubble bath I've listed ten steps to the perfect bubble bath break.

1. Make sure the tub is clean.
2. Put out clean towels.
3. Fill the bath with hot water and bubbles or bath salts.
4. Place candles around the room for effect.
5. Pour a glass of his or her favorite wine or beverage.
6. Place his or her favorite magazine or book within reach along with a hand towel to dry his or her hands before reading.
7. Fix a plate of his or her favorite snack.
8. Set up a CD or cassette player with soothing music.
9. Unplug the phone.
10. Disappear for an hour and let him or her enjoy the peace and quiet.

After the bath, you will find him or her relieved, reinvigorated, and relaxed.

~

Give your partner
a bubble bath break tonight.

Do Re Mi

Joy

~

SING! SING HIM A LOVE SONG. Sing her a lullaby. I've been singing for years in various groups and Kevin and I met at a dance party after one of my performances.

It doesn't matter if you think you can't sing. When we began dating, Kevin sang along with the radio and I told him, "I'm glad that the fact that you can't sing doesn't keep you from trying." And I meant it. It makes me feel special when he sings to me.

But I was right! We found out later when he took a series of aptitude tests that tone and pitch are very difficult for him to discern. Still, he keeps singing.

For our wedding, Kevin wanted to surprise me by singing a love song to me. With the help of a friend, he found a wonderful tune by John Lennon called "Grow Old with Me." He took voice lessons on the sly for a couple months to spice up his singing voice. However, three weeks before the wedding he got a sore throat and decided that he wouldn't be able to do a solo, so he told me about the song and included me in the surprise. We sang the song as a duet to each other at our wedding. It was the highlight of the ceremony.

~

Even now, music is a meaningful part of our lives.

Sometimes I sing a lullaby to Kevin at night.

It creates a special time together.

"Grow Old with Me"

Grow old along with me
The best is yet to be
When our time has come
We will be as one
God bless our love
God bless our love

Grow old along with me
Two branches of one tree
Face the setting sun
When the day is done
God bless our love
God bless our love

Spending our lives together
Man and Wife together
World without end
World without end

Grow old along with me
Whatever fate decrees
We will see it through
For our love is true
God bless our love
God bless our love

John Lennon

Words and music by John Lennon. © 1982 LENONO MUSIC. All rights controlled and administered by EMI Blackwood Music Inc. All Rights Reserved. International Copyright Secured. Used by permission.

Facial Art

Kevin

~

JOY AND I TOOK A COUPLES' COMMUNICATIONS COURSE and one of
the classes was about having fun. The next time you're around
little kids, take a look at their faces as they play. Our task was to
try and recapture the look and feeling of kids at play.

First, we played some silly kids' games as a group. Then the
instructor brought out a box of kids' toys. We went around the
room choosing the toys we wanted to play with.

These were simple toys, such as balls, puzzles, and games.
Joy and I were intrigued by the paint set. After we had all chosen
the toy we wanted, we were sent off to other rooms to play for an
hour. Upon closer inspection, we had selected face paints.

Joy and I giggled as we talked about what to paint on each
other's faces. Clowns seemed too trite, so we selected animals. I
painted Joy as a kitten. Joy painted me to be a puppy.

For the rest of the hour we played on the floor acting out our
parts. We tussled and romped and crawled around on all fours
making lots of noise. The instructor rushed into the room at one
point to see what all the fuss was. She laughed uproariously when
she saw what we had done.

~

Get some face paints and play.

We're sure you'll have a great time.

Meow! Ruff!

Inspected By

Kevin

~

I LOVE IT WHEN I SEE JOY coming in from the drycleaners with all of her nice clothes wrapped in plastic to be hung in the closet. It's another opportunity to be romantic.

Once she's hung everything in the closet I wait until the coast is clear and put a little slip of paper in one of her pockets.

- Inspected by Kevin, he loves you!
- To have this garment re-inspected, call Kevin.
- This garment comes with a bonus kiss, collect from Kevin.
- The inspector of this garment cares—about YOU!

Joy doesn't always find them right away but when she does it's great to see her face light up. If I'm not around, I usually get a phone call pretty quickly.

The funniest part is when Joy doesn't find the note and the drycleaner does. They usually have a big grin when they see her walk in the door.

~

Conduct your own inspections
and make sure to leave a note.
Your partner will be glad you did.

Window Decorations

Joy

~

KEVIN GOT INTO ONE OF HIS CLEANING MOODS one Sunday afternoon and cleaned the sliding glass doors in our kitchen, inside and out. They look out on the backyard where spring is in full bloom. We have a beautiful azalea bush right by the door and I take time to admire it whenever I'm in the kitchen. The clean glass made the view even more beautiful, and I said to myself, "What a thoughtful husband I have, to make my world a little brighter, without my even asking!"

Turns out he had an ulterior motive—romantic, of course! After dinner a few days later, we were talking about going for a walk. It had been storming earlier, and I asked Kevin if it had stopped raining. Kevin said, "I can't tell from here, why don't you check it out from the kitchen?" So I did, and reported back that the rain had indeed stopped. Kevin asked, "Did you check both doors?" Then I knew something was up, and looked closer. Sure enough, there was something strange on the far door. It was a love note, painted in symbols and bright colors.

Wow! I'm pretty oblivious—one of those people who see what they expect to see, and I needed a little help seeing beyond that. But it was worth it!

~

Get some Crayola washable markers and paint your own romantic window decorations. Draw a picture, compose a poem, or write your own special note. A little bit of imagination can create a lot of romance!

Glow in the Dark

Kevin

~

A FRIEND TOLD ME she had used glow in the dark chalk to write a special message to her honey. I liked the idea and set out to get my own glow in the dark chalk to try it. The toy store I went to only had glow in the dark paint, so I decided to try it. While Joy was at her aerobics class I got out my paints and wrote "I love you Joy" on the ceiling and left the light on. Joy got home late from her class and was very tired. She took just enough time to remove her contacts and brush her teeth before going to bed. Oops! I hadn't thought about the contact issue. This was going to be less of a surprise than I wanted! I found her glasses and gave them to her. "What are these for?" she asked. She was in bed with the lights out and couldn't understand why she needed her glasses. I told her there was something she just had to see. She put on her glasses and said, "Where?" "Look up" I said and she finally saw the message I left for her.

She gazed at the ceiling for a long time and a tremendous smile came over her face. She leaned over, gave me big kiss, and said "I love you." The fluorescence in the message I wrote was starting to fade by then but the glow on Joy's face lit up the night.

~

Make your ceiling and your mate glow!

Surprise Lunch

Joy

~

ONE DAY I CALLED UP KEVIN'S BOSS and asked her to schedule a noon meeting with Kevin on Wednesday. My plan was to show up and take Kevin out to lunch instead. She was happy to be my co-conspirator.

Kevin came home that evening and said his boss wanted to meet with him. What could she want to talk about? I suppressed a grin.

On Wednesday morning the projects that Kevin was working on all seemed to be in crisis mode. Kevin paged his boss that their lunch meeting was in jeopardy. She called him and ordered him to show up for lunch, "If anyone has a problem with it they can talk to me!" she growled.

Just before noon I parked in the circle in front of his office and found Kevin walking across the courtyard. The look on his face was one I want to remember—a mixture of confusion, surprise, and happiness to see me. I explained to him that his boss wouldn't be joining us for lunch! We kissed and laughed, and then I took him to a nearby restaurant for a romantic midweek getaway.

I loved sharing a romantic interlude with Kevin in the middle of his hectic workday, but most of all I loved being able to surprise him!

~

Call your partner's boss and make them your
co-conspirator for a romantic lunch, matinee movie,
or even an early afternoon getaway.

Pillow Presents

Kevin

~

JOY'S FAMILY has a grand tradition of leaving little gifts under a pillow to be found at bedtime. Pillow presents can be inexpensive or extravagant, and for any occasion.

Here is a list of ideas for perfect pillow presents:

- chocolate
- ankle bracelets
- love notes
- book of romantic poems
- movie tickets
- CD

Occasions we have used are:

- birthdays
- special anniversaries
- Valentine's Day
- Christmas Eve
- just because

Each time I find a pillow present it's special to me; and it inspires pleasant dreams as I drift off to sleep.

~

Remember to look under your pillow
before going to sleep each evening.

Romantic Poem a Day

Cody G., Washington

~

I HAVE MADE A HABIT of sending a romantic poem a day to my wife through e-mail. Each day I'm working, I find a low point in activities and search the Web for a new romantic poem, or I'll make up an original one. Usually first thing in the morning works best as the day's activities haven't picked up yet. After picking out a poem, I attach it as a personal message to a virtual post card from one of the countless virtual postcard sites on the Net.

My wife has come to expect these little thoughts of romance. It gives her a daily pick-me-up after dealing with our three boys all day long. It also helps to remind me of what's really important in my life.

~

Use the Internet to let someone know you're thinking

of them. You can send a quick e-mail, a poem,

or a virtual card as Cody suggested.

Check the Appendix for more virtual card resources.

Joy

Sunshine Squad

Kevin

I HAD REACHED ONE of those stretches at work when all I seemed to do was get up while it was still dark and go to work, then go home in the dark after a full day and go to bed. While I concentrated so hard on work I was neglecting the most important person to me—Joy. I felt bad about having so much work to do, and because my relationship was suffering. Until I got a voicemail message.

"Hello, this is the leader of the Sunshine Squad. It has come to our attention that you have not been getting your daily dose of sunshine. You are directed to appear at the front door of your office building at noon today for mandatory sunshine dosage. I, as leader, will meet you there and administer the appropriate medicine."

I scrambled to clear my schedule for lunch. I certainly didn't want to miss taking my medicine. At noon I went to the front door and found Joy waiting with a picnic basket and the top down on her car. She asked me if I knew of a park nearby where she could make sure I was getting my medicine. I sure did. We went to a park I know of that was once a thriving amusement park. We sat at a picnic table and ate while watching the old carousel that still runs there, filled with children on a field trip getting their doses of sunshine. The air was filled with giggles, laughs, and calliope music.

After we ate we rode the carousel. We held hands as our horses went up and down. After our outing I returned to work refreshed. I still remember fondly the day The Sunshine Squad took me away.

~

*We hereby deputize you as a member
in good standing of the Sunshine Squad.
We order you to ensure your mate is getting
the appropriate daily dose of sunshine
and empower you to administer it
when necessary!*

Buff Bodies

Joy

~

ONE OF MY PERENNIAL New Year's resolutions is to start exercising and lose some weight. But I find it hard to do alone and personal trainers are really expensive. Instead, Kevin and I have started working out together. How can getting hot and sweaty together be romantic?

Working out relieves stress and keeps us both healthy. We feel better about ourselves, and each other. It gives us time together to connect and talk, and we are much more motivated to stick with it. We encourage each other as we do our exercises and that carries over to other areas of our relationship.

Here are some tips to make the most of your joint workouts:

- Leave disputes at home, at least for the duration of the workout. You may find that the exercise helps clear your head and diffuses the tension.
- Find an activity you both enjoy, or alternate who gets to choose. Some great activities for couples are tandem biking, walking, dancing (if it's fast-paced), and canoeing.
- Remember that men and women are different, so don't compare yourselves with each other. Men tend to see results faster than women, and are generally stronger. Set your own goals and encourage each other to work toward them.

Hidden Kisses

Joy

HERSHEY'S KISSES combine two of our favorite things—kisses and chocolate. They are just right for a bite of sweet, delicious chocolate, and perfect for gift giving. And now they've added Hugs (white chocolate kisses), too. They can be packaged in all sorts of romantic ways:

- put a handful in tissue paper and tie it with a bow
- fill a mug with them
- decorate a cake or cookies with them
- fill a gift box with them and bury a smaller gift inside for a kiss treasure hunt

Kevin even pasted them on my poster board-sized Valentine's Day card!

One of our favorite ideas was suggested to us by my aunt Alma. Get a bag of Kisses and/or Hugs and hide them one at a time throughout the house. Then as your mate finds them they can enjoy a sweet treat and think about how thoughtful you are, or tell him or her they can be redeemed for a hug or a kiss! Some ideas for hiding places are:

- on a bookshelf
- on the shelf in a closet
- in a kitchen cabinet
- in the pocket of a favorite shirt hanging in the closet
- in the spice rack

- in each dresser drawer
- in the medicine chest
- inside the dishwasher
- in the refrigerator
- in the freezer
- in the kitchen drawer with the silverware
- in the diskette box

~

Use Kisses and Hugs to get kisses and hugs,

it's a sweet way to be romantic.

Get Out of the Rut

Kevin

~

AFTER BEING MARRIED A WHILE, I noticed Joy and I developing a standard menu of dishes to prepare for each other. Joy agreed we were getting in a recipe rut. She began looking for new recipes to try and add to our repertoire. I, on the other hand, wanted to make our new recipe journey an adventure that included romance.

While visiting a friend's office I saw a stack of cards advertising a personal chef, John LoBuglio. Every once in a while Joy needs a break from the kitchen and I thought letting someone else do the work for one night would be a really romantic gift. So I called John and we talked about menus, styles of cooking, and prices. After considering my options with John and romantic impact with Joy, I decided to have him prepare meals for us for two weeks instead of just one night.

John sent me a questionnaire about our food preferences. Joy and I filled it out and faxed it back making special notes about our dislikes, but leaving lots of room for John to be creative with the ingredients that we like. We arranged for John to come on a Saturday morning and spend the day cooking. He brought everything with him! Pots and pans and food and spices were all carried in and the kitchen quickly filled with marvelous smells. Joy and I went out to run errands while John prepared and packaged twenty meals for us to eat over the next two weeks.

The meals were delicious; it felt like we were sitting down to eat at a gourmet restaurant every day. Our favorite meal was the Tequila Lime Grilled Chicken with Black Bean and Papaya salsa. John allowed us to include the recipes for you in our book.

But the best part was that Joy didn't have to spend hours planning and preparing meals, which left her more time and energy to spend on other things, like lighting candles, arranging flowers, and turning down the lights to create a romantic dinner for two. And after dinner instead of cleaning up we could adjourn to the living room for some cuddling.

Here are tips for hiring your own personal chef summarized from *www.HireaChef.com*:

Educate yourself about the types of services a personal chef provides and understand your options. Making an informed decision after establishing your requirements will give you the best opportunity for a successful personal chef experience.

Questions to ask:

What is your background? Experience in cooking is an obvious requirement—but is it doing the types of cooking you desire?

Are you bonded and do you carry liability insurance? Your personal chef will be coming into your home to cook and an accident may happen. Know that you and your chef are covered.

Are you affiliated with a professional organization? John is affiliated with the United States Personal Chef Association and conducts his business in a professional manner.

Do you have references, testimonials, and or endorsements from clients and can I contact some of them?

What is your process for determining my requirements, food preferences, and dislikes?

Do you have sample menus I can review?

~

Only after all your questions have been answered
to your satisfaction should you hire a personal chef.
Do your homework to establish a fruitful, fulfilling,
and satisfying relationship with your personal chef.

Sporting Romance

Joy

〜

THIS TIP IS FOR ANYONE whose mate is a sports fan; use your creativity to find your own way to make it romantic.

October is the month for baseball. First, the four division championships are played; the next week, the two league championships are played; finally, the World Series—the culmination of the year's baseball season—is played.

My husband is a baseball fan.

I could resent him for spending a lot of time watching the games on TV instead of spending time with me. Instead, I thought up a romantic idea that would allow me to spend some time with him.

Anyone who's been to a baseball game knows that there are three crucial ingredients to every visit to the ballpark: hot dogs, Cracker Jacks, and the beverage of your choice. I prepared to give Kevin the ballpark experience at home.

As the game started I took hot dog and beverage orders. Around the sixth inning we shared a box of Cracker Jacks for dessert. During the seventh inning stretch we both stood up and sang "Take Me Out to the Ball Game."

At the end of nine innings the score was tied and the excitement grew with each pitch. I didn't watch the entire game with Kevin, but I was proud of myself for being there with my sweetheart when the game ended in the fifteenth inning with a dramatic grand slam home run for the home team.

〜

Hit a grand slam on the field of romance
and share sports with your love.

Surprise Picnic

Lael H., Florida

~

LAST FRIDAY WAS THE BEGINNING OF MY SPRING BREAK. When I came home my husband met me at the door with a tote bag packed with a blanket, a kite, and a rose. Was I surprised! He took me to a garden where we attempted to fly the kite in a gusty wind. After awhile my husband suggested I lay the blanket out and we could watch the clouds roll by. Imagine my shock when I unrolled the blanket and there was a bottle of wine inside and underneath the blanket I found strawberries, whipped cream, shortcake, grapes, and a card. My husband beamed as I squealed with delight. He then served me strawberry shortcake and a glass of wine before he toasted our love. Then he pulled out a book of love poetry and began reading to me while feeding me grapes.

That night we made a lovely supper together and the next day he took me to a winery where we enjoyed a tour and wine tasting. This was one of the happiest weekends of my life. I know I am so blessed to have such a loving romantic man to love and pamper me. I love him with all my heart!

~

Get outside with your partner. Hold hands while going for a walk, have a picnic together, or just lay in the grass together watching the clouds go by.

Treasure Hunting

Joy

~

FOR A FUN WEEKEND check out some local yard sales. You may find a few hidden treasures, and of course, some romance, too!

- On Friday night, go through the classifieds and circle the ads that look interesting.
- Get out a good map of your area and plan your itinerary.
- Get an early start on Saturday, but do not show up earlier than the time indicated in the ad.
- Wear comfortable clothes, make sure your wallets are stocked with dollar bills, take plenty of water and some snacks.

When Kevin and I went yard sale-ing, we enjoyed browsing through the knick-knacks and imagining what sort of history they had. We laughed together over the whatsamajig that neither of us could figure out. I squealed with delight upon discovering a book I had loved as a child.

Our best purchase of the day was a set of two bed trays. Hopefully we will have many romantic breakfasts-in-bed using them and remembering how we acquired them.

~

Plan your own yard sale adventure,

and go treasure. hunting.

Enchanted Evenings

Kevin

~

THE HOLIDAY SEASON IS A WONDERFUL TIME OF YEAR. One of our favorite evening activities is looking at the holiday light displays that crop up all around town. It's a romantic setting for a walk or a drive.

I dug out a thermos that had been sitting in storage all year and filled it with hot chocolate, grabbed two travel mugs, and off we set, after bundling up warmly. We started in our own neighborhood and walked for a while, enjoying the neighborhood displays. We stayed warm with hot chocolate and kisses.

Eventually we ran out of hot chocolate and went back to the house for the car. We drove to a special light display area where the park service decorates and charges admission to see the light show. We finished our evening with a trip to a nearby restaurant with a great big fireplace to warm us up. Soon we were feeling cozy and romantic in front of the fire.

Create your own enchanted romantic evening; you don't have to wait for winter to do it:

Fireworks—you probably don't get a chance to view fireworks very often, so take advantage when you can. Scope out a good vantage point in advance. A boat on the water is a great place to see the show. Have snacks and drinks on hand, and create your own fireworks afterwards.

Inspiration Point—every town has a quiet place to park and make out.

City lights—wander among the streets and buildings aglow with lights. Stop in a café for a drink. A water fountain all lit up at night is magical. Visit your local monument. The city sights we don't even notice during the day come alive at night.

Blanket under the stars—drive away from the city lights and find a quiet field. Spread a blanket and lie down under the stars. Have a second blanket to snuggle under if it gets chilly. Share some wine and some conversation.

~

Whether it's hot or cold outside,

you can create an enchanted evening for two.

Slicing and Dicing
in the French Quarter

Joy

~

IF THE WAY TO A MAN'S HEART is through his stomach, what better way to stir up some romance than to take a cooking class together?

That's exactly what Kevin and I did when we visited New Orleans, famous for its Cajun cuisine! We were fortunate to be able to attend a class at the New Orleans School of Cooking.

Our chef instructor was knowledgeable and entertaining. He showed us how to make jambalaya, gumbo filé, piña colada bread pudding, and pralines. He lectured about the food, the history, and the culture of New Orleans. Various students were invited to help him with his demonstrations.

The best part of the class was being able to feast on the finished products. They were superb! The unique spices added a special flavor to the food and our date.

In order to complete the class, you have to try the recipes at home and then send in a letter to get your graduation certificate.

It was a great way to sample the local cuisine and take some of it home with us.

~

Why not check out cooking classes
near you and sign up for a culinary
adventure for two!

Part Five

Baby Makes Three
(Romance after Kids)

"Love's Philosophy"

The fountains mingle with the river
And the rivers with the Ocean,
The winds of Heaven mix for ever
With a sweet emotion;
Nothing in the world is single:
All things by a law divine
In one spirit meet and mingle.
Why not I with thine?
See the mountains kiss high Heaven
And the waves clasp one another;
No sister-flower would be forgiven
If it disdained its brother;
And the sunlight clasps the earth
And the moonbeams kiss the sea:
What is all this sweet work worth
If thou kiss not me?

Percy Bysshe Shelley

Our Baby Story

Joy

WHEN I FOUND OUT I WAS PREGNANT, my first thought was, "How do I tell Kevin?" I couldn't wait to tell him! But that night we had a meeting to attend with some friends, and we wouldn't get a chance to be alone until later. All through the meeting I tried to keep my grinning to a minimum and do business as usual.

After the meeting, we drove home in our separate cars. Kevin was going to pick up some groceries, so I had time to stop by a bookstore and pick up a copy of *The Father's Almanac* by S. Adams Sullivan.

When Kevin got home, I told him to close his eyes and hold out his hands, and I got the book out of hiding. He opened his eyes and stared blankly at the book. "You're going to need it," I explained. It took him a moment to grasp the meaning of what I had just said. "You mean . . . you . . . we . . . ?" "Yes!" And the celebration of the next nine months began.

Kevin accompanied me to most of my medical appointments. It was important to me for him to be there and to be involved. Especially the first time we heard the baby's heartbeat—wow! The next day I found a wave file on the Net with the sound of a heartbeat and sent it to Kevin at the office. He loved it and programmed his computer to play it often.

Time flew by and before we knew it we were in a labor room in the hospital. Kevin was wonderfully supportive, massaging my back, and feeding me ice chips. After Ben was born and I was recovering on the hospital bed, Kevin pulled out a gift box for me. Inside was a fine gold chain with two charms on it. One was a gold cutout of a little boy, and the other was a gold cutout that said "Mom." It was perfect, and very expressive of the love we felt for each other and our new baby. Later I had Ben's name and birth date engraved on the little boy charm. I wear it almost all the time.

Less than two years later, Kevin added a little girl charm to my necklace the day Annika was born. We chose a birthing center for our second child, with a midwife in attendance. It was very calm and relaxing, and the perfect place to welcome our daughter into this world. Afterward, the midwife left us alone for awhile, so Kevin and I could share our wonder and joy. It was a very intimate moment.

God has given us two beautiful, healthy children to fill our lives with work, play, and love. I have gained a new appreciation of Kevin as a parent and a partner in raising our children. And despite the challenges of parenthood, we still make time to be romantic!

Here are some creative ideas for telling him the good news:

1. Present him with a special book such as
   - *The Father's Almanac* by S. Adams Sullivan
   - *Fatherhood* by Bill Cosby
   - *Rookie Dad* by Rick Epstein
   - *Zen and the Art of Fatherhood* by Steven Lewis
   - *The Expectant Father* by Armin Brott and Jennifer Ash
2. Give him an "I'm pregnant" dessert—ice cream with a side of pickles
3. Wrap the positive test stick in a gift box, and surprise him with it
4. Replace one of the vegetables at dinner with a baby food jar of strained carrots or peas

Here are some ideas for gifts for the new mom:

1. Boy or girl pendant with chain—I bought both and returned the unused one
2. A gift certificate for maid service for a month
3. Mother and baby gift basket with lullaby music and stuffed animals for baby and bubble bath and body lotion for mom
4. A locket and chain to keep her new baby's picture close to her heart
5. A "gift of time" coupon book with coupons for:
   - Two hours of babysitting
   - House cleaning
   - Errand running
   - Cooking for the day

Lunchbox Surprise

Kevin

~

A REALLY NICE WAY TO SAY, "I love you" is to take the time to pack a lunch for that special someone. They get a good meal and realize just how thoughtful you are. It doesn't have to be fancy—it can be leftovers, a sandwich and a snack, or a special meal you prepared. Put it in a little cooler with an ice pack.

To hit the double bonus on the romance scale, tuck in a love note or a treat to surprise your mate. A candy bar, a flower, a little poem, a simple "I love you," or a small gift will make them smile with delight!

I'd been on paternity leave with Ben and on Monday I had to go back to the office for my first full week of work in a while. It was a struggle to get up and get motivated. When I finally reached the door to leave I found a lunch packed for me.

When I finally got a break for lunch, I opened the bag and on top there was a surprise! Wrapped in a plastic bag was a small gift for me. The accompanying note said "This is for daddy from Ben so you won't miss me so much at work!" It was a framed picture of my young son, which now occupies a conspicuous place on my desk.

Here are some suggestions for lunch to go:

Mexican—a tortilla wrapped around grilled and sliced chicken or beef and shredded cheese, and a side of chips and salsa.

American—tuna with mayo and dill on whole wheat, baby carrots, and celery sticks.

Light—creamy yogurt, a fresh fruit salad, and a whole wheat bagel.

Middle Eastern—pita bread stuffed with grilled chicken, tomato, cucumber, and alfafa sprouts, with a side of hummus.

~

Make your mate feel special with a lunch

that's packed specially for him.

Include a small gift and get that double bonus.

The Things I Do

Joy

I'M OFTEN DISCOURAGED about not getting a lot of work done around the house. Fortunately, Kevin understands that taking care of an infant is hard work and it changes your priorities. I decided to write down a list of everything I did in one day, with a romantic twist. At the end of the day, I presented it to Kevin with a flourish. Here is an excerpt:

What I Did Today:

1. Ben woke up, changed his diaper, changed his clothes, played Gymbo the clown.
2. Thought about how glad I am that Kevin is willing to support our family financially so I can stay home with Ben.
3. Folded and put away load of laundry while keeping Ben entertained.
4. Nursed Ben, changed his diaper.
5. Got a call from Kevin.
6. Thought about how I love hearing from Kevin during the day.
7. Made bread, cleaned up kitchen, loaded and ran dishwasher (while retrieving Tigger for Benjamin eleven times).
8. Played with Benjamin.
9. Thought about how Ben's smile reminds me of Kevin's.
10. Changed his diaper, nursed Ben, put him to sleep.

Kevin thought my list was really special. He already knew that taking care of Ben was a full-time job, and he was happy to know that I was thinking of him throughout my day.

≈

Tell your partner what you do all day.
They might be surprised at just how often you
include them in your day even when
they aren't there.

Cloud Nine

Kevin

~

I WANTED TO SURPRISE JOY with a dinner on "cloud nine" and the conditions were perfect for romance:

- Little Ben was asleep in his swing
- the lights in the room were dimmed
- romantic music played on the CD player
- the table was set with candles and flowers
- dinner was ready
- a cloud billowed all around the floor

When Joy entered the kitchen, she was astonished to find herself walking on clouds. We ate and talked and then danced to the music, with the mist swirling around our feet. It was paradise and very, very romantic!

Here's how to create the cloud: Fill a large metal bowl half full with hot water and add dry ice. Make sure the water remains hot and that the area is well ventilated. Use one gallon of hot water for every 2–4 pounds of dry ice. The smaller the size of dry ice pieces and the higher the temperature of the water, the more fog.

~

Create your own paradise in the clouds with

a romantic dinner and a bag of dry ice.

Brag Book

Kevin

~

JUST AFTER OUR SON WAS BORN I got a gift from Joy that I treasure. It's a brag book that I keep in my briefcase.

Joy took a small photo album and made a special cover for it, with the title "Daddy and Benjamin" and a photo of me holding our tiny newborn. She used a sheet of laminate over her cover and around the edges of the album cover to protect it and hold it in place. Then she filled the pages with pictures of her, us, and our son. She also put in a special love note, a romantic poem, and the words to the song we sang together at our wedding.

Every month or so Joy takes the brag book out of my briefcase and updates it with new pictures, poems, etc. I never know when she's going to update it so I am constantly surprised. And I love showing it off to my friends, or just taking it out to browse through by myself. It always brings a smile to my face!

~

Make a personal brag book for your partner. Include photos from special outings you have had together, and some thoughts on what made it special for you.

It will be something to cherish, and hopefully, update with new special memories, for a long time!

Got a Clue?
A Real-Life Romantic Mystery!

Joy

I WANTED TO INVITE KEVIN ON A DATE in a creative way. I decided to plant clues around the house and see if he could figure out where we were going. I snuck about the house quietly planting my evidence. An envelope here and there, placed just so to attract his attention without being too obvious. In each envelope there was a clue to our date:

Clue #1—a few blades of grass

Clue #2—a length of audiocassette tape

Clue #3—the instruction insert from Kevin's "Juggle Bears" set

Clue #4—the torn corner from our kitchen calendar (I had written "DATE NIGHT" on the calendar in big red letters)

Clue #5—A colorful schedule for an outdoor theater near our home

When Kevin got home, he started finding clues and wasn't sure what to do with them. The individual clues didn't make much sense. Eventually, though, he found all five envelopes and started connecting the clues. He found the "date night" on the calendar, looked up that date on the theater schedule, and his suspicions were instantly confirmed! We were going to see a performance of

> The Flying Karamazov Brothers (jugglers)
> accompanied by the National Symphony Orchestra
> (music)
> while seated on the lawn (grass)
> on Date Night (calendar)
> at the outdoor theater (schedule)
> Mystery solved!

~

Clue your mate in to a specially planned romantic date.

They'll be most happy to play detective.

Breakfast Run

Joy

～

ONE SATURDAY MORNING I woke up early (with a baby in the house, sleeping in is not exactly an option). I decided to let Kevin sleep and go get milk and bagels so we could have a special breakfast together. I left a love note on the pillow beside him, put Benjamin in his carseat, and off we went.

I had fun imagining Kevin's face when he woke up and read the message. It said, "Darling, I know how much you love fresh bagels in the morning, so Ben and I have gone to fetch you some."

Getting milk could have been just one more chore to grouse about. Turning a milk run into a romantic gesture requires only a little creativity and imagination. It's an attitude thing.

When Kevin woke up, he noticed the house was unusually quiet. Then he saw the note! When I got home, he pounced on the warm bagels—with salmon and cream cheese—just the way he likes them. Ben went back to sleep and the two of us enjoyed a romantic, quiet breakfast together. A great way to start the day!

～

Start your mate's day on a romantic note
with fresh bagels and their favorite topping.
I'll bet if you asked the baker the day before,
they'd even make you a special heart-shaped bagel.

Silence Is Golden

Kevin

~

I AM CONSTANTLY AMAZED at the changes in your life when you have children. Ben and Annika seem to grow more, learn more, and surprise us more each day. It's not any one big thing that changes but lots and lots of little things. For example, Ben had a habit of taking off his mittens as soon as we got them on no matter how cold the day was. Imagine my surprise when, one day, I went to get him out of his car seat and each little hand was mitten clad.

Annika has the brightest smile when I come in the door each evening and she gives the best hugs. She rests her head on my shoulder and pats me on the back.

I really enjoy our kids and the time I get to spend with them. One weekend, though, I got a treat of a different kind.

Joy told me that Sunday afternoon was mine to do as I wished because she was taking the kids to a friend's house to play. I watched sports on TV, knocked about the house for awhile, and, finally, headed off to the hardware store to pick up a few items. On my way home I called to see if Joy and the kids had gotten home and if they needed anything. Joy said no, just come on home. I asked how the kids were and she said "I assume they're okay or I would have heard about it." That got my attention. I headed straight for home.

Joy had left the kids at her best friend's house for the night and we had the evening free. For the first time in nearly three years, Joy and I were alone. I didn't know what to say. When I got home it was so quiet. Joy had no special plans for the evening other than to just enjoy each other's company. Wow! We talked without interruptions, read a book with words that have three syllables, and had a quiet dinner where neither of us had to slice and dice another plate of food into little bite size pieces. It really gave us a chance to reconnect and reaffirm how much we love each other.

~

Have a good friend or family member take the kids
for a night and spend a quiet evening together.
Silence is golden, and romantic.

Phantom Ball

Kevin

~

I JUST SENT IN MY CHECK for Joy and I to attend a charity ball. Every year we've gotten an invitation and I'm really looking forward to it because I get to choose the menu. I also get to choose the music, the date, location, and attire. You see this charity ball is a "phantom" charity ball to benefit the National Capital Poison Center and my check won't be spent on a single night of entertainment but will be put to good use saving lives twenty-four hours a day, seven days a week.

Having a young son has made me very aware of all the possible dangers in cabinets, closets, and outlets around the house. I've put locks, caps, and covers everywhere, but, sometimes, he still gets where he shouldn't be. That's why having free access to a poison center is a priority.

A phantom ball is just what it sounds like, no ball at all. It's a fundraising technique where you ask people to buy tickets for a ball but don't hold the ball, that way all the money goes directly to the charity and the work they do. You may have heard of the "No Dinner, Dinner" version. Joy and I will still get dressed up, have a candlelight dinner, and dance like there's no tomorrow just as if we went to a real ball. We did it last year and it was great. I got reservations for dinner at a local hotel where the restaurant is on the roof and has a great view of the capital and the monuments. Then we got a babysitter for Ben.

Joy wore a gorgeous short black party dress and I put on a coat and tie. We had a luscious soup and appetizer before a great steak dinner. Joy had a chocolate dessert while I sipped on a cup of coffee. We then went to the bar and worked off some calories dancing to the music of a versatile and talented quartet. We talked and laughed and, after a while, declared our charity ball a success. It was a great time that I look forward to repeating next year.

~

You don't have to wait for an invitation

to create your own charity ball.

Just send a check to your favorite charity

and let them know you're thinking of them

while you're dining and dancing on

a special evening for them and you.

Pocket Change

Kevin

∽

I WAS WATCHING PBS a few months ago and they had a show on with Suze Orman. Suze is a financial advisor and author of a bestselling book, *The Nine Steps to Financial Freedom*. She was talking about how to create savings from unexpected places. One idea she discussed was to always make cash purchases using bills only. Save the change in your pocket and toss it in a jar when you get home. At the end of the month empty the jar and invest your savings.

I really liked the concept and with a little twist I make it romantic. I divide my change into two containers. The first is for pennies and nickels, which I'm saving and investing for our son Benjamin. The second contains the quarters and dimes. This is for my investing. I invest in two areas. The first, is for my long-term financial goals, and the second, and most important, is for romance.

Each month I use some of the change I've saved to buy a gift for Joy. It can be:

flowers—store-bought or florist delivered (both have a big impact)

candy—she loves all kinds of chocolate

clothes—this way I choose the items I think she looks great in

Sometimes I'll divide the money and buy two small gifts. I vary the day of the month just to keep Joy surprised. It's a great way to say "I love you!"

～

Use your pocket change for savings.

It's an excellent way to find money

to invest in life and in romance!

Train Trip

Joy

~

I'VE ALWAYS ENJOYED TRAIN TRAVEL. The rhythm of the clickety-clack, being able to relax and let the train get you to your destination, watching the towns go by, and the intimacy of a sleeping compartment make for a romantic journey.

When we decided on a spur-of-the-moment trip to Myrtle Beach, taking the train seemed like a practical solution. We could avoid the long drive with Ben cooped up in his car seat, and also avoid the expensive airfare. I have to admit, though, the train appealed to me for more romantic reasons as well.

We reserved a sleeper car for the overnight trip. We knew we'd have separate bunk beds, but when we finally boarded the train we were astonished by how tiny the sleeper compartment really was. We fell into our respective beds exhausted, and let the clickety-clack and the swaying of the train rock us to sleep.

The next morning we made our way to the dining car and there my romantic expectations were fully met. We were served a complete breakfast on white linen tablecloths. There were fresh flowers on the table. I enjoyed watching the passing scenery and smiling at my sweetheart across the table. I also enjoyed the excellent service. It felt almost like we were being served breakfast in bed!

After breakfast we went back to our private compartment and our attendant rearranged the beds into two seats facing each other. That gave us a little more breathing room. We sat and talked and smooched, and before we knew it we had arrived at our destination, relaxed and ready for action.

Getting there was definitely half the fun!

~

Get ready for your own romantic train adventure. Remember to be flexible, relax, and enjoy the ride together!

Keepsake Photo Album

Kevin

~

PHOTOGRAPHS ARE PRECIOUS REMINDERS of our special times together. If you're like us, however, you may glance at them a few times, then put them away and rarely look again, storing away those memories. For a long time I had wanted to organize all the pictures Joy and I have taken together, so we could enjoy them. Well I finally did it. I couldn't get through all of the photos—but I found enough to create a wonderfully romantic album for Joy.

I started at the office supply store where I purchased one of those three-ring binders with the plastic over it so you can insert a cover page. I also got a set of drop-in plastic page protector sheets and some heavy-duty colored paper. At the local camera shop I bought special photo insert pages. Then came the hard part.

First, I collected the photos from all the different places they were stored around the house and put them in a big box. I had to do this on the sly so Joy wouldn't know what I was doing. I carried everything out to the car and took it to the office. Then at lunch and after work I started sorting out the best pictures from each of the big events over the years. There were pictures from trips, dates, and, especially, our wedding.

Next, I created a draft timeline for everything. I tried to have a few pictures from each event and loaded them into the special display sheets. I wrote a paragraph or two about my memories of what we did or how I felt at each event, printed them on the colored paper, and inserted them in the drop in sheets between the picture sheets. Writing an introduction to the album and creating a cover page for "Our Romantic Journey Together" was the final step.

When I was finally finished with the book I boxed it and wrapped it to give to Joy. I presented it to her after Ben was asleep. She oohed and ahhed over it, and we spent the rest of the evening going through the album. It was a hit!

∼

Create a keepsake of your romantic journey.

Rediscover your special memories to share together.

Take a Hike

Kevin

~

ONE OF THE WAYS THAT JOY likes to stay in shape is to walk. She'll cruise the neighborhood, usually pushing Ben in his stroller. As often as I can, I go along and we talk and plan and just spend time together. One weekend we were invited to a family picnic with an easy hike up Sugarloaf Mountain.

It seemed like the perfect opportunity to sneak some quiet romance time walking hand in hand. We even got an offer from someone to take care of Ben while we hiked!

The bright sunshine was perfect for walking to the top of a mountain. We drove out to Sugarloaf and met everyone there. Most of us decided to work up an appetite before lunch while some stayed and began picnic preparations. As the crowd spread out along the trail Joy and I had time to talk and rest and kiss on the steps near the summit. At the top we sat on the rocks and enjoyed the panoramic view. As we talked I pulled out my pocket-knife and sliced up an apple for us to share.

~

Beautiful scenery, fresh air, exercise, and romance—
what a perfect way to spend part of an afternoon.
Tell your mate to take a hike, and make sure you go
along to create your own quiet romance.

Web Page

Kevin

~

I SENT JOY AN E-MAIL that said, "Check out this Web site".

It was for a very romantic Web page beginning with the header "I Love You Joy!" followed by family photos of the two of us and our son, Benjamin. The photo was accompanied by the poem "If Thou Must Love Me," by Elizabeth Barrett Browning.

She loved it! A Web page dedicated to our love was a big romantic hit!

There are a number of sites on the Web that will allow you to build a Web page. I chose Geocities and there are others, such as Angelfire and Tripod. Most have some sort of generic Web site builder and graphics to go along with it. A quick search on Yahoo! turned up more than twenty places for free Web sites. Most of these place advertising on your page or have pop-up boxes for advertising.

I started my page with the basic Web builder at the Geocities site, and created a framework for the page. This took me about twenty minutes to complete.

Then I added some of my favorite pictures. This step and the next take just a little bit of html knowledge, but not much.

I did a search and found romantic graphics in the public domain that I could include. You can dress up your page with flashing, spinning, or otherwise animated graphics and text.

All this took about an hour. When I had it just right I sent Joy the address. What a great response for a little bit of effort.

~

Create a Web page of love for your mate today!

Just Because

Kevin

~

OUR SON BENJAMIN is a wonderful addition to our lives. Though it's not always easy—Joy quit working to stay home with him. She's great with him whether taking him to the park, to swim class, or even to the doctor. It's marvelous to get an excited phone call from her when he does something new or really cute.

One of the things Joy misses is spending time with other adults. To remedy this she formed a playgroup with five other moms that have kids within a year of Ben's age. The Playgroup Posse, as they have come to be known, gets together once a week—it's a welcome social time for each of the moms.

One week, when playgroup was at our house, I double checked the time and called a local florist. "Please deliver a dozen roses between 12:30 and 1:00 this afternoon." I timed this for maximum effect when all the moms would be there.

The roses were beautiful and Joy was ecstatic. The other moms oohed and ahhed. They're still talking about it. I scored very high on the romance meter!

Later I got the chance for bonus points. Joy asked me why I'd sent the roses and my response was, "Just because."

There are lots of reasons to justify a "Just because" to share with your loved ones, and only you need to know. Here are a few "Just because" reasons:

- I think you're beautiful
- I'm glad you're my child's mom

- I appreciate what you do for the children and me
- I love you!

Create you own list of reasons and then do something special for her "Just because."

Evening Stroll

Kevin

~

JOY AND I OFTEN TOOK BEN out for a family stroll in the evening. But one night I decided to make it a more romantic stroll with just the two of us, so I arranged to have a neighbor look after Benjamin. At lunch time I walked to a nearby toy store to get sidewalk chalk. Sidewalk chalk comes in multiple colors and is thick in diameter to hold up while drawing on concrete.

I left work a little early to avoid traffic and stopped around the corner from the house. I called Joy to say that I was "on the road." She told me she was working on dinner and it would be ready in about a half hour. Perfect!

I started in a sidewalk block with a simple heart framing our initials. I walked about ten steps and continued with stick people holding hands, words from "Our" song, and lines from some romantic poems. Then I went home to a great dinner.

After we ate I sprung my surprise walk on her. I picked up a flashlight and we started out arm in arm. As we neared my starting point I nonchalantly played the light over the first drawing. Joy was delighted! "Aha, so you had an ulterior motive for this walk. Well, I like your motives," she said. We walked on, and enjoyed the other drawings and messages along the way.

~

Get yourself some sidewalk chalk

and give your partner a romantic evening stroll!

Clean Machine

Kevin

~

FOR THE LAST FEW WEEKS before our daughter Annika was born I did most of the driving when we went out. It was difficult for Joy to get into and out of her car which is much smaller, and there was a lot of snow and ice on the road. I was home on paternity leave for the two weeks after and did all the driving during that time also. Joy's car sat for almost a month and by that time was very dirty. The day before I had to return to work was the perfect time for an automotive display of affection.

That afternoon, while everyone else was napping, I snuck out of the house with the keys to Joy's car. First, I drove to a specialty auto shop for a quick oil change and lube job. Next, I went to the car wash and had them wash and wax and vacuum the car thoroughly. Then it was off to the gas station for a full tank of gas. Lastly, I left a mushy "I Love You" card taped to the steering wheel and rushed home so Joy wouldn't realized what I was up to.

The next day I got a call at work from an ebullient Joy. She loved the opportunity to drive a clean car and the card was icing on the cake.

~

Surprise your sweetie with a clean machine,
and don't forget the "I love you!"

Babysitter Surprise

Joy

~

I WAS OUT RUNNING ERRANDS one afternoon when my cell phone rang. It was Kevin, just checking in to say hello. Or so I thought. Very casually, Kevin mentioned he'd like to go with us to a particular store after he got home from work. The store closed at 7 P.M., so he asked me to have the kids ready to go when he arrived. I said, "What about dinner?" He mumbled something about eating later. We had talked previously about some things we needed, so I said ok. We'd just have to eat on the run that evening.

Just before the scheduled time I was rushing around getting the kids dressed and packing the diaper bag when Kevin walked in with our babysitter! Imagine my surprise!

We left Ben with the sitter and out we went for an early romantic dinner. Annika, who was only 2 weeks old, cooperated and was quiet throughout the meal. I was happy to get some "two of us" time, and it was so unexpected!

I really appreciated Kevin for making all of the arrangements for an evening out, including the babysitter! All I had to do was sit back and enjoy it. And I did.

A key ingredient for romance is preparation. For a couple with kids, babysitters are indispensable. Kevin and I are very fortunate to have a regular babysitter and a couple of backups. I keep a card with their phone numbers in my wallet and next to the phone at home.

Places you can find babysitters are in your neighborhood, at your church or synagogue, or through a local hospital.

Look for a babysitter that has taken some form of certification class. Many hospitals, high schools, and the Red Cross have classes.

Once you have a babysitter identified, there are a few more things you should do to prepare. First check references! You're asking someone to watch *your* child. Give your babysitter a complete house tour. Have an instruction sheet and review it with the babysitter. Prepare an emergency contact list with names and phone numbers and an itinerary of your plans for the evening.

~

As I said, preparation is key and the wonderful evening Kevin and I had couldn't have happened without it. Be prepared for your romantic evening and enjoy the time together without worrying about the kids.

Scavenger Hunt

Kevin

~

I FOUND AN ENVELOPE ADDRESSED to me on the keyboard of my computer. Inside was a card inviting me to a scavenger hunt. I had no idea what kind of treasure I'd be hunting but knew that Joy would make it special. I thought about asking for hints but figured that would take away from the surprise. My excitement grew as I waited for Saturday night.

On Saturday evening I got ready and Joy handed me a new card:

> Golf is tough
> With slices and flubs
> Go to the place
> Where you bought your clubs.

Off I dashed because I knew that the golf shop closed at 7 P.M. When I arrived the kindly gentleman behind the counter chastised me for being so late and then handed me a new card:

> Now find a shop near That's Amore
> That has my cousin's name
> Everybody knows it
> And the wine is still the same.

I know where That's Amore is (a restaurant near us) but I couldn't place the shop where I needed to go. Finally, I located

Norm's, a local wine shop. Inside a gracious and charming woman beamed brightly and handed me a new card:

Rice is sticky
Mangoes are sweet
Where is our favorite
Place to eat?

Cool! Thai food and mangoes and sticky rice for dessert. I raced off to the restaurant. It was bustling for a Saturday night, and I explained to the host what was going on. "Oh!" he said and reached into his reservation book. He handed me a card:

You've made it!
Hip, hip, hooray! Yahoo!
Now please join your wife
At a table for two.

We had a marvelous dinner. It was romantic and caring and fun.

Hints on setting up a scavenger hunt:

- Choose your clues. Joy used little rhymes, but you can also do word puzzles, program electronic devices, or plant physical objects. You get bonus points for creating "insider" clues, based on a private joke or ritual. Your clue locations can be around town or around the house.
- Consider timing, especially if driving distances are involved. For my scavenger hunt, timing was crucial because Joy had to coordinate the babysitter's arrival and dinner reservations along with the hunt itself.
- Make sure the place will be open during the scavenger hunt. Joy called to verify the hours the shops were open.

Then she made the cards ahead of time and distributed them a few hours before the hunt.

- Distribute the cards in reverse order that your mate will collect them. That way if there is a glitch and you can't leave a card somewhere, you can revise or leave out a clue.
- Pick places that your mate is familiar with. It's easier to make up clues that way.
- Small, one- or two-person shops are better than large ones, because you know you'll be talking to the same person that will greet your mate.
- If you are entrusting clues to strangers, put a small picture of your significant other on the back of each card so he will be easily recognized.

Part Six

Special Occasions

"Sonnet 18"

Shall I compare thee to a summer's day?
Thou art more lovely and more temperate.
Rough winds do shake the darling buds of May,
And summer's lease hath all too short a date.
Sometime too hot the eye of heaven shines,
And often is his gold complexion dimmed;
And every fair from fair sometimes declines,
By chance, or nature's changing course, untrimmed.
But thy eternal summer shall not fade
Nor lose possession of that fair thou ow'st,
Nor shall Death brag thou wand'rest in his shade
When in eternal lines to time thou grow'st
So long as men can breathe or eyes can see,
So long lives this, and this gives life to thee.

William Shakespeare

Holidays

Mid-Winter, Mid-Summer

Kevin

~

JOY AND I BOTH WERE BORN and raised in warm weather climates so we're always looking for special ways to keep warm in the winter. So here's our top five list for the coldest extremes and the warmest climates.

Winter Wonderland:
Five Ways to Keep Your Loved One Warm

1. While your mate is showering, throw his or her towel in the dryer for a few minutes, so it'll be nice and warm for drying off.
2. Make some hot chocolate and snuggle together under a warm blanket while watching a romantic movie.
3. Rent time in a hot tub for an evening. It's very invigorating!
4. Build a fire in the fireplace. If you don't have one, maybe you can borrow a friend's home for an evening. Or take your mate to a local bed and breakfast with a fireplace in your own room!
5. Be environmentally conscious and use solar power to keep your mate warm. Surprise your mate with a trip to a place with bright sunshine and warm water.

Hot, Hot, Hot!
Five Ways to Keep Your Loved One Cool in the Summer

1. Freshly made, ice cold lemonade is always a treat!
2. Wash your car(s) together, and make sure to "accidentally" spray him or her. Retaliation is encouraged.
3. Share a walk in the rain (singing is optional).
4. Spend the day at a water park. Slide down the biggest chute together, or relax on a double inner tube. Don't forget to splash each other in the wave pool!
5. Go to an air-conditioned movie theater for a triple feature. See one for him, one for her, and finish up with a romantic movie for both of you.

Halloween

Joy

~

HALLOWEEN is a great time for some creative romance! Create your own romantic Halloween costumes for a night to remember. There are three rules when creating Halloween costumes:

1. It must be easy to hold and drink a beverage.
2. Using the restroom mustn't be a chore.
3. Your costume has to be romantic.

If you don't want to spend money on an expensive, store-bought costume, there are many quick and easy ways to create a romantic costume from home. One easy idea is for a slinky black cat costume.

- Use black stockings and a black leotard as the basic costume.
- Buy some face paints and create a cat face, complete with whiskers.
- If you're feeling very adventurous, use some temporary hair color for your hair.
- A black feather boa tied around the waist makes for a perfect tail to twitch.

With a little imagination, you can be the cat's meow!

Kevin is a big guy and rather than be gruff, menacing, and scary, he becomes cute and cuddly as a bunny rabbit. He wore an old pair of gray sweats turned inside out, white socks on his hands and feet, and painted his face white. The final touches were bunny ears and a nose from a costume shop.

Other quick and easy ideas:

- **Dalmatian**—Wear white sweats and for spots, use either washable paint, or pin paper spots on. Add a white headband with white socks attached for floppy ears. Use a long white tube sock stuffed with paper for the tail. Finish with white and black face paint.
- **Train engineer**—Wear a flannel shirt, overalls, boots, bandanna, and engineer's cap.
- **Sandwich Board**—Take two pieces of posterboard and attach them together with string or ribbon so they'll hang over your shoulders. Draw something creative on the posterboard.
- **Road Signs**—Cut colored posterboard into the correct shape, yellow with "Dangerous Curves" printed in black letters or red with white "STOP" letters
- **Turtle**—Cut colored posterboard into ovals, yellow with geometric design on front and green with turtle shell markings on back.
- **M&M**—Cut colored posterboard into a circle. Cut a lowercase "m" from a piece of white paper, and glue or tape to the center of the circle.
- **King or Queen of Hearts**—Find a picture of you in profile and have it enlarged on a color copier twice and use it for the face of the king or queen.

Get in the spirit this Halloween
and dress for romantic success!

Giving Thanks

Kevin

~

AS WE ALL KNOW, Thanksgiving comes in the fall, and it is a good time for all of us to remember and acknowledge the things we are thankful for.

I am thankful for the romantic relationship that I have with my wife Joy and I've compiled a list of ten things in our relationship for which I am thankful.

1. I can disagree with her and she respects my position but doesn't feel obligated to change hers to accommodate me.
2. She is intelligent and has common sense.
3. She is beautiful without being self-absorbed.
4. She is a good cook.
5. She is adventurous.
6. Joy tolerates my baseball and golf obsessions.
7. She has a pretty voice and sings to me.
8. Joy understands when I work long hours and doesn't demand all of my time.
9. She is unafraid to show her love for me.
10. Joy is the mother of my children, and I am most thankful for that.

It's all too easy to get caught up in day-to-day activities and begin to take your relationship for granted. It's very important for you and your mate to step back and appreciate the great things your relationship and romance bring into your life. It's also important for you to tell your partner how you feel.

~

For your next Thanksgiving, come up with a list of ten things you are thankful for about your partner and share them on Thanksgiving and throughout the year.

Holiday Gift-Giving

Kevin

~

THE HOLIDAY SEASON was just beginning when I read an article by Michelle Singletary in the *Washington Post* about the stress of gift-giving: She only wants exactly the gift she has asked for. Michelle's husband feels that it spoils the spirit of giving if there's no surprise. Is this a man thing? Joy and I propose an essential holiday gift-giving rule: Don't get stressed out!

Men and women can both win! So your mate hand-picked their present—this doesn't mean you can't add mystery or romance by wrapping it uniquely or delivering it in an uncommon way. Say she wants a pair of earrings. Wrap the box inside a bigger wrapped box inside a bigger wrapped box, and so on, until she has no idea what you're giving her.

Or say he wants a new CD player. Buy it, but don't stop there! The creative gift-giving has just begun! Buy three of his favorite CDs and host a holiday scavenger hunt.

- Wrap the player and hide it somewhere in the house.
- Take the first CD, along with a note telling him where the player is, wrap it and hide it somewhere else in the house.
- Take the second CD and wrap it along with directions to the first CD and hide it also.
- Finally, take the third CD and directions to second CD, wrap them and place them under the tree.

Joy and I play a game to help us select gifts for each other. This is a great way to get a wish list out of a reluctant (or not so reluctant) partner. Play a game called "Romantic, Practical, or No." To prepare, get a pad of paper, and a catalog or some store sales brochures. Browse through the catalog or brochures. As you reach each new category ask him if he thinks it is Romantic, Practical, or No as a gift for you. Tell him what you think, then do the reverse and guess whether you think it is Romantic, Practical, or No for him. Talk about why.

Voilá! You each have gift lists to pick and choose from. You may also want to have a list of things not in any catalog, such as dinner out, tickets to a show, vacation places, etc.

Joy and I used this game to develop a "yes" and "no" list of romantic gifts for the holidays. We had great fun and came up with a list of potential gifts for each other that will last a long time.

~

Play a gift-guessing game with your sweetie.

You're sure to end up with warm holiday

hugs and a lot less stress.

Last-Minute Gift Ideas

Joy and Kevin

~

IF CHRISTMAS IS CLOSING IN and that perfect gift is still eluding you, here is a quick list of ten easy last minute gift ideas ranging from inexpensive to exotic:

1. **Chocolate**—Kisses and Hugs from Hershey's are always well received. If your sweetie is a chocolate lover, surprise them with a month's supply! Godiva, Ghiradelli, or Fannie May are also good chocolate choices.
2. **Music**—Music can be a great romantic gift—especially if you use a little insight. Next time you're at your sweetie's, check out their music collection and make a quick mental list of the artists you see. Choose a CD by an artist from your list that you didn't see in your sweetie's collection.
3. **Flowers**—The vivid colors and scents of flowers add a festive touch to any room. Combine red roses or white carnations with seasonal greens such as holly, ivy, mistletoe, rosemary, bay, or evergreens. Most florists offer beautiful seasonal arrangements, perhaps dotted with candy canes, or nestled in a sleigh. Or consider a poinsettia plant, which will last throughout the season.
4. **Videos**—Movies and romance are made for each other! What better way to spend an evening than curling up together with a bowl of popcorn? Discover your sweetie's favorite flick and buy a copy for a gift that keeps on giving.
5. **Fragrance**—Scents are a popular romantic gift. A perfume or cologne that smells great on the saleswoman in

the store may not be so alluring on your mate due to the subtle differences in body chemistry. A great way to avoid this is to take your partner along with you and test fragrances together.

6. **Jewelry**—Long dangling earrings, bracelets, and necklaces are all good choices. A classic gold chain is simple, elegant, and very wearable.

7. **Cookies**—Homemade holiday cookies are a traditional, well-received gift. Even if you're not a gourmet chef, there are plenty of simple cookie recipes for the holidays, from sugar cookies to that old stand by—chocolate chip! Sharing cookies and a glass of milk with your sweetie on Christmas morning can be very romantic.

8. **Literature**—For an inexpensive yet romantic gift that will score you major points in the mate department, why not memorize a romantic poem for your mate? Practice reciting it out loud. Take the printed poem and roll it up like a scroll. Tie a bow around it with red ribbon. If you're having a hard time finding a poem, choose one from this book.

9. **Travel**—Buy your loved one a cruise to someplace warm. There are many types of romantic cruises that can brighten a bleak winter.

10. **Something Red**—A red phone, or a red faceplate for your partner's mobile phone. You can say that it's a hotline direct to your heart.

Holiday Gift Receiving Guide

Joy

~

NOW THAT YOU'RE PRIMED to make the perfect holiday purchase, it's important that you remember how to receive your gifts. Have you ever heard one of the following:

- I can't believe you bought me *that*!
- That color looks terrible on me.
- It's not what I asked for.
- You spent too much on that.

In Ellen Kreidman's book *Light His Fire*, she advises, "Appreciate the man, not the gift." This indispensable advice works for both genders.

When you open that long-awaited wrapped box, if it's exactly what you wanted, great! If it's not, think about the time and effort put into buying your gift—surly sales clerks, bulky Web sites, fighting holiday traffic, and the hard earned money that your mate spent choosing that perfect gift for you. Your relationship is more important than the gift itself, so tell him how lucky you are to have him and how special you feel when he picks something out just for you.

~

Show your mate that you appreciate

the gift by using it.

Twelve Days of Christmas

Joy

IN THE BUSTLE OF THE HOLIDAYS, it's common to have a to-do list that's a mile long. Take the time this year to show the one you love how much you care by giving a gift for each of the twelve days of Christmas!

With this unique idea, Christmas doesn't have to be a one-day-only event. A great way to remind your favorite person that you are thinking of them each day during the holiday season is to celebrate the twelve days of Christmas. The twelve days of Christmas actually start on Christmas day, but you can celebrate early and enjoy the holidays even longer! Gather twelve small Christmas tree ornaments and celebrate the "Twelve Days of Christmas" early.

You can make the ornaments yourself or buy them from your favorite store. There are plenty of easy to make ornament kits at most craft stores. Each day, give your sweetie one ornament with a personal note. Give it to them in person, or hide the gift as a surprise.

The gifts don't have to be ornaments—bath items (good for pampering!) or chocolates make wonderful pre-Christmas gifts. This fun and easy idea will help keep the holiday spirit, as well as the romance, alive for a long time.

Ornaments

Joy

∼

AH, THE SMELLS OF THE HOLIDAYS—pine needles, peppermint, and cinnamon. The aroma of cinnamon reminds me of good things from the kitchen—yummy, hot, and gooey glazed cinnamon rolls or hot spiced cider with a cinnamon stick. It's amazing to me how just a whiff of these smells can overwhelm me with warm, romantic, and cozy feelings of home.

One Saturday, Kevin needed to run some errands in the morning so it was the perfect time for Ben and I to make something special for him in the kitchen. I knew that by the time he got home the scent of cinnamon would fill the air. After I cleared the counters, Ben climbed onto the stool, and we began by dumping a whole bottle of cinnamon into a bowl. A friend had given me a recipe for tree ornaments made with cinnamon (the recipe follows below). It was really fun and easy.

Needless to say, the kitchen smelled wonderful right from the start. We made the dough, rolled it out and Ben had a grand time with the cookie cutters. He even sang "Twinkle Twinkle Little Star" as he cut out some star shapes. I set aside one heart shape to decorate later.

Just before Kevin got home I went back to my heart ornament and etched a special holiday message on it using a toothpick: "JD + KD." I couldn't wait to give it to Kevin.

Cinnamon Ornaments
Each batch makes approximately 15–20
(depending on how thick you make them)

Ingredients:
A 2.37-ounce (67 g) bottle of cinnamon
Applesauce
Rolling Pin
Cookie Cutters
Paper towels
Cookie sheet
1 drinking straw
¼" ribbon

1. Take the bottle of cinnamon and empty it into a bowl. Start with ¼ cup of applesauce and mix the applesauce into the cinnamon using a fork. If it is too dry, add more applesauce. It should be the consistency of dough.
2. After the mixture is mixed together, roll the mixture into a ball and knead it with your hands for ten minutes. The more you knead or "play" with it, the smoother it will become and the nicer it is. If it is too wet, add more cinnamon.
3. Sprinkle some cinnamon on a flat surface. Use your rolling pin to roll it out (like sugar cookies). Cut out shapes with cookie cutters. Transfer "cookies" onto paper towel lined cookie sheets. Use the drinking straw to make a hole in the top of your "cookie." Let dry for two days.
4. After "cookies" are dry, take off the rough edges with your fingers or knife. String cookies with ¼" ribbon. They smell wonderful! Store them in an airtight container so the smell lasts longer.

Hint: Start off with a little less applesauce first. It is easier to add more applesauce if it is too dry then to add more cinnamon if it is too wet (for some reason, adding more cinnamon does not always work if it is too wet.)

When Kevin walked in the door he was overwhelmed with the smell of cinnamon. Kevin said it was extra special because I had Ben help me. Not an easy task when dealing with a two-year-old. He went right out to get our tree so he could hang our new ornaments near the top. It's a romantic gift that we will treasure for years to come.

〜

Use a little spice to create your own special ornament this year. It will be a keepsake you can use and treasure every year.

I Resolve . . .

Kevin

∽

START OFF THE NEW YEAR RIGHT! Instead of the usual promises about diet and exercise, why not include romance in your list of resolutions? With a little creativity, this resolution is one you'll definitely want to keep!

I resolved to give Joy a ten second kiss whenever I got home at the end of the day. I heard about the concept from a book by Ellen Kreidman called *The Ten Second Kiss*. I tried it out intermittently over a few weeks with great success. I'm not sure Joy realized exactly what was happening but the responses I got were along the lines of "Oh my!" or "Wow" or "Mmmm." I noticed her physical response too. It went from three or four seconds of surface tension to a couple of seconds of slight resistance to a release and melting into each other's arms. It was Great! I highly recommend it. Here are some other simply romantic resolutions:

1. Kiss each other every day before you go to work.
2. Say "I love you" to your mate before going to bed each night.
3. Call your partner at least once a day to say "I love you."
4. Bring home flowers once a month just because.
5. Go to a movie or show once a month, just the two of you.
6. Memorize the words to your partner's favorite poem and recite it while on a date.

7. Sign up for a fun class together like cooking, massage, dancing, etc.
8. Turn off the TV once a week to kiss, talk, hug, or snuggle.
9. Dress up for dinner once a month.
10. Hold hands when you are out together.

∽

Use one of our resolutions or come up

with a romantic resolution of your own.

Just make sure to follow through and you can

make the coming year the most romantic ever!

Valentine's Day

Classified Romance

Kevin

~

JOY IS IN A SINGING GROUP that performs a concert series for the December holidays. Each concert series has a program with advertising to support the group. I remember showing up for a holiday concert one year. As the usher handed me my program everyone around me grew silent. They already knew that Joy had placed an ad in the program to tell me that she loved me. When I found the ad I felt very special. You can create that special feeling for your partner with a simple phone call.

Check on classified rates in your paper. Ask about special rates for holidays like Valentine's Day, Christmas, or New Year's Day. Our local paper runs a special section on many holidays. You can make up your own romantic saying or quote a line from her favorite poem or song.

~

Joy knows to check the paper on holidays!
Call your local paper today and get your ad
in the classifieds for your next special occasion.

Feeling Lucky

Joy

~

ONE OF KEVIN'S NICKNAMES for me is Lucky. I tell people it's because I'm lucky to have him. So I decided to surprise him with a lucky lottery ticket for Valentine's Day. I even found one that had a "Lucky Valentine" theme. I tucked it into his lunch bag and imagined the smile on his face when he found it.

Kevin laughed when he opened his lunch and saw the ticket on top. It made his day lucky indeed, even before he scratched the surface.

~

Buy a lottery ticket this week and hide it for your sweetheart to find. If tickets aren't available to you, or it's against your principles, create your own! Small gestures like these, and the unexpected surprise it creates, can turn an ordinary day into something special. And who knows, you may get really lucky if it turns out to be a winner!

Take a Romantic Portrait of the One You Love!

Kevin

FOR VALENTINE'S DAY, what better way to show your affection than to take a romantic portrait of the one you love? Here are five tips from photographer Chuck DeLaney, dean of the world's largest photography school—the New York Institute of Photography (NYIP)—to help you do it right.

1. You want the focus of attention in your photo to be your subject's face and expression. Suggest dark clothing that will be subdued—avoid checks, stripes, and big patterns, unless such outfits are your subject's trademark. The subject's face should stand out, not the clothing!
2. Come in close and fill the frame with your subject. Generally, you'll be better off with a "head-and-shoulders" shot in which the hands don't show.
3. If the hands do show, give them something to hold—gloves, a small bouquet, a hat—anything that's appropriate.
4. Use a relatively fast film—outdoors: ISO 200: indoors: ISO 400, or faster. Shoot some pictures with flash, some without.
5. When using a flash, keep your subject a few feet from the background to minimize dark wall shadows.

List reprinted with permission by Chuck DeLaney, Dean of the New York Institute of Photography.

Of course, when you get back the prints, examine them carefully. Then take the best photo, have it enlarged, and tastefully frame it for a great Valentine's Day present!

~

For more ideas on taking great pictures, take a look at the NYIP Web site or the Web sites of most of the camera and film companies. Shoot it, print it, and frame it for a great picture of romance.

Snail Mail Cachet

Kevin

~

ONE OF THE TRICKS I've learned to help me be romantic is to keep a few funny romance cards in my briefcase. I also keep a mushy one or two because they seem to have an even bigger impact. I will occasionally pop a card in the mail for no reason other than the fact that I'm thinking about Joy and want her to know she's on my mind.

Valentine's Day is the perfect time for sending cards to your sweetie. To make it more special try remailing it. Huh? You may be asking, "What's remailing?"

There are certain cities in the United States that have a romantic postmark: Loveland, Colorado, and Valentine, Nebraska are two of these. They both provide a remailing service that works like this: You send them your card in a preaddressed and stamped envelope inside a larger envelope. They open the larger envelope, take out the smaller one and "Remail" it. Of course that means a new cancellation mark and a card postmarked from Loveland or Valentine, delivered straight to your valentine.

Note that this is a *free* service! Pick up a card and remail it. Your sweetie will be glad you did!

Loveland, Colorado

To receive a unique cancellation and Valentine cachet, just enclose your prestamped, preaddressed Valentines in a larger First Class envelope and mail it to the following address.

Postmaster
Attn: Valentines
USPS
Loveland, CO 80538-9998

Your Valentines will be removed from that envelope and hand stamped with the Loveland cachet, then cancelled at the Loveland Post Office.

To ensure delivery by Valentine's Day, U.S.–destined mail must be received by February 9th, and foreign destined mail must be received by February 3rd at the Loveland Post Office.

Valentine, Nebraska

If you would like to send special greetings with the special "Valentine" postmark, address your card as you would if you were sending the card from your location, stamp and all. Place your card into a larger envelope and mail it to:

Cupid's Mailbox
P.O. Box 201
Valentine, NE 69201

To have your cards delivered by February 14th, they need to be delivered to Cupid's mailbox by Monday, February 5th. All letters received after this date will still receive the cachet but might not be delivered until after Valentine's Day. The Post Office will start sending out stamped letters on Monday, February 5th.

How Do I Love Thee?
Let Me Count the Balloons

Dave M., Kentucky

~

A MEN'S GROUP AT OUR CHURCH coordinated a secret Valentine's Day dinner—a week before Valentine's Day, so none of our wives would suspect. Somehow, I was able to keep our night out and all my preparations a secret—Linda didn't suspect anything.

The night before our surprise date, I had written out 100 different things that I love about Linda on 3" x 5" index cards. Some of them were general things that any head-over-heels husband might write about his wife, like "You mean everything to me," and "You're the only woman that I even notice,"—not to imply that I didn't mean every one of them. And some of them were things that most other people wouldn't catch on to, like "I love your 'inner waitress,'" since she always straightens up the tables after we eat at a restaurant; and "Just Because," which is what she wants to name her band, if she ever has one.

On the afternoon of our date, I stuffed her car with 100 red, pink, and white balloons. Inside each balloon was one of the index cards with another reason that I love her. There were so many balloons inside her car, that you couldn't see anything else—it was a challenge to get them all inside and still be able to close the doors!

On the window, I taped a note saying that we were going on out a special date, and that she should pop the balloons to find out why. Attached to the note was a safety pin. The note also said that she should go home and put on a nice outfit, then meet me at the Holiday Inn for a night of dinner and music, and that I had arranged a babysitter to take care of our son.

Linda walked out after work and noticed something strange about her car. When she saw the balloons and read the note, she was so excited! Her friends were in the know and had accompanied her, and they all set to work popping and reading. The security guard came to investigate and said, "This is the most romantic thing I have ever heard of." He insisted on cleaning up the mess in the parking lot when they were all done, so Linda could get going.

When Linda walked into the hotel she looked stunning. I gave her a sweet kiss, and told her how beautiful she looked. Then I escorted her to our room! We were spending the night. I had arranged flowers in the room and left sparkling cider chilling. We had a glass of cider, and then went down for dinner.

She noticed another couple from our church in the lobby. That's when I explained about the secret dinner. Not long into the dinner, one of our dear friends came over to our table and asked me if I pulled it off. This opened the story up to the table. Within minutes, the story was floating around. Women were coming over saying how jealous they were, and men were congratulating me on a job well done.

～

Balloons are colorful, fun, and romantic. One time Kevin filled our living room with balloons while I was out with our son Benjamin. We returned to a sea of balloons and Ben and I had a grand time popping them all. Kevin had hidden a dinner invitation in just one balloon, so when I saw it I felt like I had found buried treasure!

Joy

Valentines by the Dozen

Joy

~

ONCE WHEN WE WERE DATING, Kevin gave me the most charming Valentine's Day greeting. When I opened my front door to leave for work, I discovered that Kevin had sneaked over during the night and decorated my door with dozens of little Valentine's Day cards, each with a special message!

The cards meant a lot to me. I enjoyed taking the time to untape each one and read the message. I may have been late for work, but it was a Valentine's gift I'll never forget!

This is an easy and inexpensive idea to implement. Visit a local card shop in the six weeks that lead up to Valentine's Day and you're bound to find boxes of Valentine's Day cards for kids. I'm sure you've seen them with a variety of current or classic comic characters. Winnie the Pooh seems to be very popular in our area.

~

Other possible options are to leave valentines on the windshield of his or her car or around the house in unexpected places. Overwhelm your Valentine with kids' cards but make sure each has a note to make it extra special!

Take Stock

Kevin

~

THERE ARE MANY THINGS that say romance such as candy, cards, or flowers. Another thing that says romance is commitment to the long term in your relationship. A few years ago, I got Joy a Valentine's Day gift combining both candy and a long-term commitment.

I bought Joy shares of Hershey (HSY) stock! Joy loves their Kisses and Hugs almost as much as mine. I purchased enough shares to enroll in the Direct Stock Purchase Plan (DSPP) and qualify for free dividend reinvestment. That way, when Hershey pays out a quarterly dividend, more shares are purchased and the account builds over time. With a DSPP the company holds the shares and sends you updates on a monthly or quarterly basis.

You can also add to your Kisses and Hugs by making small additional payments and helping to grow your value over time.

Other romantic stocks you might consider are:

- Ben & Jerry's Ice Cream (BJICA)
- Victoria's Secret (Intimate Brands) (IBI)
- Royal Caribbean Lines (RCL)
- Tiffany (TIF)
- USA Floral (ROSI)

You don't have to have a brokerage account, some companies will let you invest directly either through a DSPP or Dividend Reinvestment Plan (DRIP). If the cost of a DSPP or

DRIP is not in your budget you can still buy a share to give your sweetie (pun intended).

~

There are a few companies that specialize in one share of stock as a gift. You can even have them frame it for you. Invest in your relationship with shares of romantic stocks.

Last-Minute Valentine

Joy

~

OKAY, SO IT'S THE DAY BEFORE VALENTINE'S DAY and you're desperate for a last minute idea. Try this tip for a quick fix and a memorable Valentine's Day:

Using your music collection, find some music that you can slow dance to. Wrap it up and give it to your mate with a note inviting them to spend the evening with you dancing cheek to cheek. Order a gourmet meal (takeout or delivery) from your favorite restaurant. Don't forget candles for mood lighting!

Don't worry if you don't know any fancy footwork. Just stand together and sway to the music gently. Your partner will love it and so will you.

Other last-minute ideas:

- Pick up a few inexpensive prepackaged bouquets at the grocery store. Remove the plastic and wrap the flowers together with a festive ribbon.
- Make a homemade card.
- Melt a bag of chocolate chips and dip whatever you have available: fruit, cookies, or nuts. Arrange on a tray and serve.

~

Sometimes you just have to be spontaneous!

More Super
Than Supersize, and Bigger
Than Biggie Fries!

Joy

THIS IS YOUR CHANCE TO BE CREATIVE, revert to your childhood, and impress your partner with a handmade original! Create your own giant Valentine to give to your sweetheart! You will need:

- one piece of white or red posterboard
- a bag of candy hearts (you know, the kind with little sayings on them, like "Hug Me")
- posterboard
- markers in various colors
- scissors
- colored construction paper
- glue
- heart-shaped doilies
- ribbon

1. Arrange the candy hearts in a heart shape in the center of your card and glue them to the poster. In the middle write a short Valentine poem using the markers. Cut paper hearts out of construction paper by folding the paper in half, and cutting out a half-heart shape.

2. Unfold the paper, and voilá, a perfectly symmetrical heart! Glue paper hearts and doilies to the poster. Continue decorating with ribbons (the curly kind look nice), markers, cutouts, glitter, or anything else you like until you have created an extravaganza of love. Make it really showy!

~

If you really want to show it off, have it delivered to his workplace, or tape it to his or her front door. Make your partner feel very special with your own giant Valentine's Day card.

Birthdays

Happy Birthday?

Joy

~

I ONCE HELPED KEVIN CELEBRATE a "virtual birthday." It wasn't his actual birthday, but I pretended that it was, and made it a special day for him. In the morning I made him a special omelet for breakfast and left a "Happy Virtual Birthday" card next to his plate. He wasn't quite sure what that meant, but he said it sounded like fun.

I hid presents around the house for him to find in the afternoon, and that evening I booked a babysitter so we could go out for a nice dinner. It was a great day and it was fun to fill it with Kevin's favorite things and make him feel special from morning to night.

You can give your mate a virtual birthday anytime. It can be a substitute if you won't be together for his real birthday, or it's too close to a major holiday.

Here are some ideas for celebrating:

- Order a bouquet of balloons.
- Share a banana split.
- Make him his favorite meal.
- Tell everyone you meet that it's his birthday.
- Let him sleep late.

~

Give your mate a virtual birthday.

Coupon Clipper

Joy

~

KEVIN'S ROMANCE COUPON

Redeem this coupon for

A Passionate Kiss

At your choice of date, place, and time
before the expiration date of
__ __ / __ __ / 2 0 __ __

WOW! WHAT A THOUGHTFUL GIFT Kevin gave me for my birthday.
A coupon booklet filled with love and romance, and very personal! There were coupons for all sorts of treats—a back rub,
dinner at my favorite restaurant—all the things that Kevin knows
I like. And we both had fun using the coupons. I'm hoping for a
reprint for my next birthday.

KEVIN'S ROMANCE COUPON

Redeem this coupon for

A night at the ballet

At your choice of date, place, and time
before the expiration date of
__ __ / __ __ / 2 0 __ __

This is a simple, yet effective, way to demonstrate your love for your mate. And it lets them participate in the romance by choosing the date, time, and place for the event.

KEVIN'S ROMANCE COUPON

Redeem this coupon for

A romantic candlelight dinner

At your choice of date, place, and time
before the expiration date of
_ _ / _ _ / 2 0 _ _

To create your own coupons you can modify these, fill a page with them, print out a coupon sheet and give it to your partner. Another option is to get some 3" x 5" cards, fill out a dozen or so and give them to your mate. One more idea is to use a small notepad and fill in each sheet as a coupon. Your partner can then just tear off a page to redeem it.

Here are twenty-five ideas for coupons to get you started.

1. A picnic
2. Movie tickets
3. Sporting event tickets
4. Wash your car
5. Back rub
6. Candlelight dinner
7. Dinner at your favorite restaurant
8. Adventure dinner at an ethnic restaurant
9. Walk in the park
10. A new car (rented for the day or weekend)
11. Dinner and dancing

12. Kisses
13. Hugs
14. Serenade of your favorite song
15. A new book from your favorite author
16. A new CD from your favorite artist
17. Flowers
18. Candles
19. A teddy bear
20. Renting a favorite video
21. An evening playing your favorite game
22. A box of your favorite chocolates
23. Share of stock in a romance company
24. Subscription to your favorite magazine
25. Shampoo your hair

Make your own Personal Romance Coupons.
You can also find Web sites on the Internet
that will help you fill out and print coupons
or e-mail them to your love.

PPFs (Migrating Flock)

Kevin

~

THEY TRIED TO BAN THEM IN VIRGINIA. Their healing powers have been recognized in Texas where they've also been the victims of senseless violence. They've even been altered to help in scientific research in Florida. What am I talking about?

Why, PPFs or Plastic Pink Flamingos.

And what do PPFs have to do with romance? Just ask Joy. For her birthday, I once "flocked" her.

A local youth group was doing "flockings" to raise money for a trip they had planned. For a rental fee of $2 per bird they would show up late at night and plant a flock of flamingos in the yard with a special message.

On Tuesday morning Joy walked out of the house to find the yard filled with a flock of pink flamingos and a birthday message hung on the neck of the bird closest to the house.

It was totally unexpected and Joy's flamingos were the talk of the neighborhood. She still got a card and a nice dinner, but she'll always remember the birthday when she got flocked with pink flamingos.

~

A quick search on the Web will find sites where you can order the supplies to do your own flocking or have a flocking done for you. For a bold, creative, and romantic birthday gift try flocking her!

Birthday Stamps

Sonia D., Pennsylvania

~

MY HUSBAND STEVE knew I wanted a big bash for my fortieth birthday. I didn't expect to be surprised, because I'm usually pretty good at figuring out what Steve is up to. This time, however, he planned a series of surprises that topped anything I could imagine.

On the morning of my birthday, he told me to pack my overnight bag. My sister, Sylvia, had been visiting us for five days and was leaving after lunch. I was getting ready to wave goodbye to her when Steve told me I was going with her! I had a wonderful time talking with Sylvia on the 120-mile trip to our Uncle Gary's house.

Later in the afternoon, two more sisters showed up at Uncle Gary's house. Joy lives nearby but Sandra had flown in all the way from California! Wow! Steve must have been working double time to arrange that. He knows how much I value time with my sisters, whom I don't see very often. Another marvelous surprise!

At supper time Steve showed up too. Surprised again! He hired a babysitter to care for our two boys. I was very happy with Steve's surprises but he wasn't done yet! After supper our hosts said we had to clear the table quickly for "the next activity."

It turned out to be a "Stampin' Up!" party—something I'd been wanting very much. It's a party where they demonstrate and sell rubber stamps, ink, and special paper supplies. A few months earlier I had actually asked Steve if we could host a "Stampin'

Up!" party on my birthday. He didn't think much of the idea, so I shelved it. I was totally surprised!

We had a wonderful evening. Steve and I had a night without kids and a lovely romantic trip home the next morning. Now every time I use my rubber stamps, I will think of Steve's love for me.

~

Way to go, Steve! A series of surprises

is always fun because it's even more surprising.

How can you surprise your partner?

It's the Thought
That Counts

Kevin

~

JOY'S BIRTHDAY WAS COMING UP and I was talking with her about what sort of gift she'd like. She told me, "I don't care if you give me ping-pong balls, it's the thought that counts." Of course I had already picked out a nice bracelet but I couldn't let the romantic opportunity go by.

I went out and bought a very nice card and a dozen ping-pong balls. I very carefully sliced open one of the balls and placed the bracelet inside. Using a small piece of clear tape I resealed the ball and wrapped it in a box with the others.

The night of her birthday we went out to dinner. After we ordered I brought out the box. "Happy Birthday, Joy!" I exclaimed, and handed over her present. She very carefully opened the box, looked inside, and set it aside, laughing.

"I love you," she said with a beautiful smile. We sat and talked for a while and then I told her to take another look at the ping-pong balls. As she opened the box it slipped and ping-pong balls bounced all over the restaurant. Once we had finally corralled them, Joy began looking at the ping-pong balls a second time.

The last ball was the special one and she shook it to try and figure out its contents. When she opened it her smile was even bigger.

~

*Get three ping-pong balls and one Hershey's Kiss
or Hug. Open one of the balls and place the chocolate
inside. Seal the ball and then all three together
in paper and ribbon. Surprise your mate with the gift
one night and enjoy the happy smile you get in return.
Remember—it's the thought that counts!*

Wake Up Call

Joy

~

I NORMALLY WAKE UP EARLY during the week to take care of the kids but one morning was special. It was my birthday and I knew that Kevin would take care of the kids for as long as possible, letting me get just a little more rest.

I lay in bed and drifted in and out of sleep when I heard "Joy, I love you . . . Joy, I love you . . . Joy, I love you." What the heck? I glanced over to the nightstand to see a picture of Kevin and the kids on a little clock and it was speaking to me. It was a talking photo frame/travel alarm clock. What it said was not the time, but "I love you" in Kevin's swoon-inducing bass voice.

Now when I wake up in the morning it's my sweetheart's voice reminding me that he loves me. What a way to start the day!

~

This would make an especially nice gift
if your mate travels a lot, or if you two
are in a long-distance relationship.
You can rerecord a message anytime, or even pass it
back and forth alternating messages.
The talking photo frame/travel alarm clock
is available from Brookstone.

Splurge

Kevin and Joy

~

MY MOM ALWAYS TOLD ME that everything should be done in moderation but I think that every once in a while you should splurge. Splurges can come in all shapes and sizes. Don't worry! Splurges don't have to be expensive.

Like the time that Joy sent a limousine to pick me up for a date. I was happy, impressed, romanced, and luxuriated for a week after.

Or the time that Kevin told me that we were going to a local beach for the weekend and we ended up in a condo in St. Thomas. Now *that* is getting away! I loved every minute of our romantic stay. It was great to spend time together and concentrate on only each other.

Or the time that I was out of town for my birthday and Joy sent me a two pound package of green M&Ms. I don't know how many bags she had to sort through to get them but I was impressed, highly sweetened, and thoroughly "aphrodisiac'd."

Or the time that Kevin saved up to get me an emerald necklace. He stopped by early in the morning on my birthday and gave it to me, telling me that he wanted me to be able to show it off at work. I had to change clothes to match my new necklace and was almost late for work.

Splurge! Give her five dozen carnations,
send him twenty humorous romantic cards, use a whole
roll of film taking pictures of him in your favorite outfit,
or give her five pounds of her favorite chocolate.
It's a great way to romance the person you love and
show them how much you care.

Set in Stone

Kevin

~

JOY'S BIRTHDAY WAS COMING and I discovered a really cool romantic gift. I found a kids' toy catalog with a kit for concrete paving stones. I plan to create three stones. One will have Joy's and my handprints and our wedding date. The other two are going to have our kids' hand and footprints along with the date they were born. Like I said, really cool!

One of the nice things about this gift is you can get the kids involved. Let them use their imagination as they add color and texture to their design. You can use:

- paint
- mosaic tiles
- glitter
- polished stones, marbles, or pebbles
- stained glass
- leaves, flowers, and ferns (leave them in the concrete—they can be washed out in about two weeks, leaving only the impression)
- seashells

You can make your own stones, or buy a kit. Make sure any sharp edges are embedded in the concrete so the stone will be smooth enough for bare feet.

~

Create a lasting token of your love for your sweetie.
They will never get a more concrete show of affection.

Anniversaries

Wedding Anniversary Gifts

Kevin

~

THE TRADITIONAL LIST OF GIFTS for each wedding anniversary has been around for more than 100 years—its origin is unknown. The list indicates a different category year by year until the fifteenth anniversary and then increments by five years.

In 1937, the American National Retail Jeweler Association issued a more comprehensive list, the Modern List. Most references will provide you both lists and there are many on the Web.

When you reach your fiftieth anniversary and each anniversary after you can arrange for a presidential greeting. Contact the White House Greetings Office for more details and do it early. They require at least a six-week advance notice for processing your request.

The Queen of England sends congratulatory messages to British citizens and citizens of the Commonwealth Realms celebrating their sixtieth, sixty-fifth, and seventieth wedding anniversaries and every year thereafter. Write at least three weeks in advance of the anniversary or birthday to request an application form. British citizens should address letters to: The Anniversaries Office, Buckingham Palace, London SW1A 1AA. Citizens of Commonwealth realms should apply via their Governor-General's office. A copy of the relevant marriage certificate is required.

Traditional Gifts

YEAR	GIFT
First Year	Paper
Second Year	Cotton
Third Year	Leather
Fourth Year	Fruit/Flowers
Fifth Year	Wood
Sixth Year	Candy/Iron
Seventh Year	Wool/Copper
Eighth Year	Bronze/Pottery
Ninth Year	Pottery/Willow
Tenth Year	Tin/Aluminum
Eleventh Year	Steel
Twelfth Year	Silk/Linen
Thirteenth Year	Lace
Fourteenth Year	Ivory
Fifteenth Year	Crystal
Twentieth Year	China
Twenty-Fifth Year	Silver
Thirtieth Year	Pearl
Thirty-Fifth Year	Coral
Fortieth Year	Ruby
Forty-Fifth Year	Sapphire
Fiftieth Year	Gold
Fifty-Fifth Year	Emerald
Sixtieth Year	Diamond

Modern Gifts

YEAR	GIFT
First Year	Clocks
Second Year	China
Third Year	Crystal/Glass
Fourth Year	Appliances
Fifth Year	Silverware
Sixth Year	Candy/Iron
Seventh Year	Desk Sets
Eighth Year	Bronze/Pottery
Ninth Year	Linen/Lace
Tenth Year	Leather
Eleventh Year	Jewelry
Twelfth Year	Pearls
Thirteenth Year	Textiles/Furs
Fourteenth Year	Gold Jewelry
Fifteenth Year	Watches
Twentieth Year	Platinum
Twenty-Fifth Year	Silver
Thirtieth Year	Diamond
Thirty-Fifth Year	Jade
Fortieth Year	Ruby
Forty-Fifth Year	Sapphire
Fiftieth Year	Gold
Fifty-Fifth Year	Emerald
Sixtieth Year	Diamonds

Firsts

Kevin

~

WE RECEIVE MANY E-MAILS from our readers asking for ideas for special occasions and one of the more popular questions is about first anniversaries. Joy and I sat down and talked about how to make a first anniversary special. We propose a special day with three meaningful paper gifts (paper is the traditional first anniversary gift).

1. Arrive at her doorstep just before dawn, wake her and give her the first present of the day. A small wrapped gift box with notepaper inside that says "My gift to you is the first ray of sunlight this morning. It represents to me how you light up my life." Following this up with a nice breakfast will start the day on the right note.
2. Before leaving for the day kiss her and tell her this is her second gift. Explain to her "This is the first of a million kisses." Then give her a scroll that says—"Redeemable for 999,999 more kisses." She'll certainly spend the day thinking about you and look forward to seeing you again later in the day.
3. A special dinner is certainly appropriate. Try to time it so it ends just before sunset. Take her outside, look up at the sky, and wait for the first star to appear. Tell her "My last gift to you on our first anniversary is the first star we see tonight. It represents how you are a wish come true for me." Present her with a scroll decorated

with your names, the date, hearts, stars, and the words
from the children's rhyme about wishing on a star,

~

Add creativity, thought, and meaning to make

a piece of paper romantic for your first anniversary.

Swing Coach/First Anniversary

Kevin

~

IT WAS THE MORNING OF OUR FIRST ANNIVERSARY and we were in Myrtle Beach. Instead of sitting on the beach, I was standing on the driving range at golf school. My bride was on the next tee and Eddie, the golf pro and instructor, was working with her on her swing. I had been playing for a long time and she was just starting, so we kept Eddie on his toes.

It was one of those days that you want to bottle and keep and reopen later when you need a lift. Joy and I had time to play golf in those days, but now things are different. I still get out once in awhile to play but Ben and Annika keep Joy pretty busy these days. For now working on her game is a lower priority.

When we do get the chance to play together we enjoy it, but it can cause some stress for me. Because our ability levels are so different I'm always in a quandary. Just how much advice should I give?

I found help in a magazine article by a local LPGA pro, Leslie Guttenberg. It was called "Coaching Your Partner," and it had the following quiz she uses at her couple's workshops.

1. Playing with my partner is:

   a. A chance to spend quality time together.
   b. More fun than I thought it would be.
   c. The highlight of my week.
   d. Ruining our relationship.

2.   The thing that bothers me most about playing with my partner is:

   a.   The pace of play.
   b.   The unsolicited advice.
   c.   The lack of patience.
   d.   The difference in our ability levels.

3.   I want my partner to play golf with me because:

   a.   It's a chance to spend time together in beautiful settings.
   b.   It's a chance to socialize with other couples.
   c.   It's a sport we can play together.
   d.   It's an opportunity to spend time together and compete.
   e.   I won't feel guilty when I go to the golf course.

4.   On the subject of giving advice, I wish my partner would:

   a.   Keep his or her mouth shut.
   b.   Be more patient.
   c.   Only give advice when I ask for it.
   d.   Help me more often.
   e.   Listen to me.

There are no right or wrong answers to this quiz. Most couples have the same or very similar concerns when playing together. When preparing for a round, ask two simple questions:

1. Do you want to be coached today?

    For the best results take Leslie's advice "Limit the advice and increase the encouragement."

2. What do you want this day to be about?

    Men and women tend to have very different goals when playing. Agreeing beforehand on what you're trying to accomplish and making a plan for it sets the tone for a good round.

As always, communication is the key.
Choose together to have a romantic round
of golf and you will.

Quiz reprinted with permission by Leslie Guttenberg. Printed as an article entitled "Coaching Your Partner," *Pros N' Hackers* magazine, June 2002.

Bed and Breakfast/Second Anniversary

Kevin

~

WE CELEBRATED OUR SECOND ANNIVERSARY by going to Thistle Hill Bed and Breakfast near Skyline Drive in the Blue Ridge Mountains. The scenery was beautiful and the weather perfect.

We arrived after a two-hour drive through the country just in time for afternoon tea on the front porch. Cookies and small sandwiches complemented a variety of teas. We nibbled, sipped tea, and talked about the years since we were married and our visions of the future. Sated and content, we went to our cozy room. I read and napped until getting ready for dinner. Joy took a long hot bubble bath in the garden tub under a bathroom skylight.

While most bed and breakfast owners concentrate on unforgettable breakfasts, Thistle Hill also has a marvelous restaurant open for dinner. Joy and I were seated next to the fireplace, which gave a warm glow to the meal. The food was exquisite and the service was fantastic.

The next morning we got up late (being able to get out of the normal routine is a special treat) and went to breakfast. Pancakes made by the owner along with fresh juice, muffins, and scrambled eggs started our day off right.

~

*Going to bed and breakfast inns can provide
a wonderful opportunity to connect with each other
without the usual distractions of day-to-day life.
Research some bed and breakfasts in your area.
Select one to visit and make a reservation to go soon!*

Beads for Baubles/Third Anniversary

Kevin

OUR THIRD ANNIVERSARY was approaching and I was on the lookout for a special gift for Joy. The third anniversary is "leather." I know Joy appreciates thought, creativity, and originality more than dollars and glitz.

I was browsing through a craft store when I saw these really neat kits for making bracelets and necklaces with lettered beads. I bought a kit and took it home.

I made a simple bracelet with a loop at one end and double knot at the other that fastens through the loop. The beads spell out "Joy" and "Kevin" with a heart in between. When she opened the bracelet she put it on immediately. I was really happy to see the smile on her face.

Make a gift for your mate. Simple crafts can be so meaningful with your own special touch. Find some inspiration at a craft store or use one of these ideas:

- Wear your heart on his sleeve: Use fabric paints to design your own romance art on a T-shirt. Sign the back with your handprints.
- Mobile: Use letters and die-cut shapes hung on a string to declare your love.
- Decoupage: Decoupage a jewelry box with photos and words of love.
- Knock on wood: Paint a heart-shaped stool or rack in bright colors.

Sand Writings/Third Anniversary

Joy

~

FOR OUR THIRD ANNIVERSARY, Kevin and I rented an oceanfront condo at Myrtle Beach, one of our favorite vacation spots. I loved opening up the door to the balcony, walking out and soaking in the sights, sounds, and smell of the ocean. We were only a few floors up so we had a good view.

On the morning of our anniversary, I was up early with Benjamin. Kevin was still asleep, so I decided to go out for a walk and prepare a special anniversary surprise. I put Ben in the stroller and off we went—a few steps and we were on the beach. I turned to locate our balcony—fortunately, we had put out some towels, which helped to identify it.

I found a large stick and smoothed out the patch of sand right in front of our condo. It was still slightly damp from the high tide, which was on its way out. I started writing, hoping I was making the letters large enough to read, but not so large that I would run out of room. My message read: Happy Anniversary, Kevin! I Love You!

I looked at my handiwork, smiled, and strolled off down the beach with Benjamin, enjoying the morning breeze. When I got back to the condo, Kevin had just gotten up and was making breakfast.

I couldn't wait. Yet even when I took him by the hand and led him out onto the balcony he didn't see anything extraordinary. I laughed and pointed downward. Finally he got the message. I got a big kiss as well as a "happy anniversary" before we went back inside for breakfast. It was the perfect start to a great anniversary.

~

Next time you are at the beach,

write a special message to your mate.

Or you can always use the sandbox

in a local park!

Gift of Time/Fourth Anniversary

Joy

I AWOKE EARLY ON THE MORNING of our fourth anniversary. I slipped out of bed and padded into the kitchen for some juice. I moved as quietly as possible trying not to wake the rest of the house. When I opened the refrigerator door I had to rub my sleepy eyes to make sure I wasn't seeing things. What I did see, even on second look, was an envelope propped against the juice carton with my name on it!

I placed the envelope on the table, poured my juice, and sat down to enjoy them together. Inside the envelope was a beautiful anniversary card, which said lots of mushy stuff that made my little heart go pitter-patter. What a great way to start our special day. Later on Kevin asked how I liked the card. I told him how much I like the mushy stuff. He said, "Oh, you didn't read far enough." I got the card out again and looked closer. Aha! There was something written on the back of the card.

"The traditional fourth anniversary gift is flowers. For our fourth anniversary my gift to you is four hours helping plant a flower garden in the front yard next spring. Happy anniversary!"

What a great idea; I loved it! Flowers for a day are nice but Kevin's gift of time, and a flower garden, will keep our anniversary spirit alive all year long.

~

There are lots of terrific ways to spend time together.
Take a class together, stroll through the park, play a
game, or share a good book. Give your mate the gift of
time and keep your romantic spirit alive.

Fun in the Sun/Fifth Anniversary

Kevin

~

OUR FIFTH ANNIVERSARY was approaching and I wanted to make it special for Joy. The traditional fifth anniversary gift is wood—the modern is silverware. After a lot of thought I finally decided to go with wood and add a unique twist. I bought a wooden key fob that had Joy's name carved into it and attached the key for a new convertible that I'd rented.

Pre-kids, Joy drove a very cool blue Mazda Miata convertible. Joy loved to drive that car in the countryside on winding roads with the top down and the wind blowing through her hair. Now it's just not practical.

I planned to rent her a Miata for the day. After checking around I found that's not an easy thing to do. I can rent a Porsche Boxster convertible, a Mercedes convertible, or even a Jaguar, but no Miata. The major car rental companies only have Chevrolets, Chryslers, or Fords. I thought the Boxster would be fun but the $650 for the weekend seemed a bit pricey. I ended up reserving a Chrysler Sebring convertible.

Joy loved it! I watched the kids for the afternoon while she was driving. It was a special way for her to get some time to herself and recharge. Rent a car and find romance.

~

*Most of the major car rental companies
have convertibles for rent. You'll have to pay a premium,
however, and they're not available in all locations.
Check with your chosen company for more information.*

Memory Box

Michelle J., Wisconsin

❧

I WANTED TO SHARE AN IDEA for a recent gift that I gave to my husband for our fifteenth anniversary. I'm always knocking myself out trying to find the perfect gift for him. However this year, I tried to do something really special that didn't cost much. I got the idea of a "Memory Box" somewhere off the Internet. But I went a little farther with the idea to make it gift-worthy.

I took one of those cardboard school pencil boxes and sponge painted it inside and out with a dark maroon and then a metallic gold paint (acrylic craft paint).

I made a list of many of the memories that we have made together. I then typed up each memory in great detail and printed it out on Ivory Parchment Paper. I tore all 4 sides of the paper to make rough edges and to make it look like an old scroll. Then I took one of those gold metallic paint pens and outlined all the way around the edge of the paper.

I rolled the paper around a pencil to get it nice and small and tied the scroll up with a metallic gold ribbon. I put all the scrolls inside the box, put a hole in the front of the box and top of the box and tied it closed with another ribbon.

A note attached to the box said, "Nothing that I could purchase could add up to all the wonderful gifts you have given me . . . you have given me so many great memories. So that is what I'm giving to you, all of my wonderful memories of things you did, and how they made me feel."

Some of the memories were romantic and some were funny.

- The first time I signed my name using his last name.
- Saying good-bye when he left for the Air Force.
- The first time he said "I love you."
- The night we met.
- Our first kiss.
- His proposal.
- Some of the more daring things we did before kids.
- When we were driving to our honeymoon destination, and my pillow accidentally flew out the car window.

I came up with about twenty-five of them to fill the box. Honestly, I was a little embarrassed to give it to him, because it was so inexpensive and kind of corny. But when I gave it to him, we sat down and read them all together. You could see which ones touched him the most as he struggled to hold back tears. But after he read the last one, he literally broke down and said that it was the best gift he had ever received. My husband is one of those macho, hold your feelings in, kind of guys, so it was very touching.

All of the materials were purchased at Wal-Mart and my total cost was less than $10.

≈

Make your own memory box and add your own special touches. There are lots of different materials you can use. This is really a gift from the heart and that is what's important.

Offbeat Anniversaries

Joy

〜

WHEN YOU'RE PART OF A COUPLE, you know there are certain days in your relationship that must be celebrated. If you are married, you have to celebrate your anniversary. Birthdays are mandatory and Valentine's Day is a must!

Don't limit yourself to only the "big" occasions! There are lots of other romantic days to celebrate as well!

Kevin took me on a special date to the ballet one night, and as we were walking into the Kennedy Center, he asked me if I knew what day it was. "March 20," I replied. "And what happened on March 20 a year ago?" he asked. It took me a moment to remember—it was the day I fell in love with him!

On March 20 a year before, he had also taken me to the ballet. I wore black, we flirted all night, and he took me home and kissed me good night. It was a special evening, and I knew then that I was head over heels for this man. Sometime later I must have told him that was the night I fell in love, but the date didn't stick in my mind. How did he remember that, when I hadn't a clue? Wow! His remembering made me feel very loved.

Imagine my surprise when I got a call at the office from my honey wishing me a happy two year and one month anniversary of our marriage. It made my day! (Hint: it doesn't have to be an anniversary, it can be a monthiversary.)

~

*Think of a calendar date that means something
to your relationship. The day you met, your first date,
your first kiss, or any other special moment.
On that date, send your partner flowers with a note
recalling the original occasion. If it is feasible, recreate
the original occasion in some way, such as dining
at the same restaurant. He will undoubtedly be
surprised and impressed that you took the time to
remember and celebrate!*

Capturing Time

Joy and Kevin

∾

TIME PASSES SO QUICKLY. The year 2000 began amid much excitement. Some say it marked the end of the millennium and some say the millennium ended the next year. Either way, it was a special new year, and we celebrated it with a time capsule tribute to our wonderful romance. We will open the capsule on our twenty-fifth wedding anniversary.

Joy and Kevin's 1999 Time Capsule contains:

- a matchbook from the bar where we met
- a Brazilian flag (Joy was born in Brazil)
- a Panamanian flag (Kevin was born in the Canal Zone, now Panama)
- a United States flag
- recipes from our first dinner
- pink beach sand from our vacation in Bermuda
- a postcard of the Washington Monument
- music from the song we sang at our wedding
- locks of our hair
- Valentino and Valentina Beanie Babies
- a polaroid picture of Joy, Kevin, and Ben with a 12/31/99 paper
- a copy of the index page from our Web site
- our joint family tree
- a menu from our favorite restaurant
- love letters to each other in envelopes sealed with a kiss!
- an inventory list of all the enclosed items

We spent the evening putting it together and sealed it just before midnight. Then we drank a toast to the New Year, our romantic time capsule, and each other. Cheers!

We made our own time capsule, but there are lots of places that you can buy one. Some are guaranteed for 500 years, not that we will be around to collect if it fails. You can even register your time capsule with the International Time Capsule Society to ensure that it's found in the future.

∽

As you end the next year, remember to celebrate your romantic memories and capture them in your own romantic time capsule. Start now on a romantic plan to build future romance!

Any Day Is a Good Day

Joy

AMERICANS LOVE HOLIDAYS. In addition to the well-known ones, such as Thanksgiving, there are many more obscure ones, such as March 22, "Goof Off Day." How, you might ask, did I know about "Goof Off Day"? I was searching the Web for an offbeat day to celebrate and found it on a great Web page. The Holidays on the Net Web site (*www.holidays.net*) has a comprehensive list of the current monthly, weekly, and daily designations.

Did you know that March is National Frozen Food Month and National Umbrella Month? Why not celebrate by sharing an ice cream sundae or taking a walk in the rain with your sweetie? There's even a week in August designated "Resurrect Romance" week. Who comes up with these holidays? I don't know, but there's an excuse for romance any day of the year; you just have to put the right spin on it.

Pick an offbeat day to celebrate. Some examples:

- March 25 is Greek Independence Day. Celebrate with Greek Pizza, rent the video "Captain Corelli's Mandolin," and dream of spending days together on a sunny Greek island.
- January 8 is Elvis Presley's birthday. Have a private party for Elvis. Play only his music, swivel those hips, and sing "Love Me Tender" to each other.

Part Seven

Romantic Recipes

Breakfast Burrito

Kevin

~

JOY AND I WERE ON AN exercise and diet program that was pretty strict six days a week. The seventh day was "free day" and we could eat anything we wanted. At times the foods we ate were decadent. The following recipe can be made in healthy and decadent versions. We frequently started our "free day" with it.

Breakfast Burrito

Ingredients
4 eggs or equivalent egg substitute
1 tablespoon chopped onion
4 ounces shredded cheddar cheese substitute
1 can refried beans
4 flour or whole-wheat tortillas
1 tablespoon sour cream
¾ cup salsa

Directions
Scramble eggs, adding onion and cheese when almost done. Spread beans on the tortillas. Add egg mixture. Top with sour cream and salsa. Roll and eat.

~

Spice up the start of your day
with a breakfast burrito.

Tequila Lime Grilled Chicken
with Black Bean
and Papaya Salsa

Joy

~

THIS IS OUR FAVORITE MEAL from our personal chef, John LoBuglio.
He graciously shared his recipe.

Tequila Lime Grilled Chicken

Ingredients
4–6 boneless, skinless chicken breasts
2 limes, juiced
4 ounces tequila
2 tablespoons garlic
2 tablespoons honey
Salt and pepper to taste
3 dashes each, Tabasco and Worcestershire sauces
1 tablespoon blended oil

Directions
Mix all ingredients together. Allow chicken to marinate for
15 to 20 minutes. Grill chicken.

Black Bean and Papaya Salsa

Ingredients

1 can black beans, drained and rinsed
3–5 tomatillos, husked, washed, and diced
1 onion, diced
2–3 tablespoons garlic, chopped and toasted
Several sprigs of cilantro, chopped
½ ripe papaya, diced
¼ cup vinegar
¼ cup sugar
1 jalapeno, minced
1 bell pepper, diced
3 dashes each, Tabasco and Worcestershire sauces
2 limes, juiced

Directions
Prepare all items as indicated on the ingredient list. Combine and allow to rest to marry flavors.

Madras Chicken

Joy

≈

VISIT SOUTHERN INDIA with this hot and spicy chicken dish. Serve it with basmati rice and a cold mango lassi (fruit smoothie) to cool your palate.

Madras Chicken

Ingredients
3 teaspoons minced fresh ginger
4 teaspoons minced garlic
1 cup water
1 teaspoon red pepper powder
½ teaspoon ground turmeric
2 tablespoons black peppercorns, coarsely crushed
½ teaspoon salt, optional
3 whole chicken breasts, skinned, boned, and cut
        into 1½-inch pieces
2 teaspoons olive oil
1 cinnamon stick, crushed
2 teaspoons cardamom
2 teaspoons curry powder
1 cup chopped onion
1 cup chopped tomatoes
½ cup sliced cucumber

Directions

1. In a food processor or blender, combine the ginger, garlic, and water and mix into a smooth paste. Add the red pepper powder, turmeric, and 1 tablespoon of crushed black pepper, and salt (if using). Rub the mixture into the chicken and marinate for an hour.

2. Heat oil over moderate heat and add cinnamon, cardamom, and curry. Stir together well and add chopped onion. Sauté for 2 minutes and reduce heat to medium. Stir in 2 tablespoons water and continue to sauté until onions are lightly browned. Add more water if necessary to keep onions from sticking to the pan and burning.

3. Increase heat to moderate and add chicken. Stir until browned on all sides. Add ½ cup water and bring to a boil. Reduce the heat to a simmer and cover for 10 minutes. Stir occasionally and add water as needed to prevent burning or sticking. Add the tomatoes and cook for 5 minutes, stirring occasionally. Add the remaining black pepper and continue cooking until meat is tender. Serve with sliced tomatoes and cucumber.

Mango Lassi

Ingredients
mangoes
yogurt
3 ice cubes

Directions
Blend 1 part mango, 2 parts plain yogurt, and 3 ice cubes for a wonderful cool sweet drink.

(Madras recipe adapted from *Indian Light Cooking* by Ruth Law.)

Indonesian Chicken
with Green Beans

Kevin

~

EARLY IN OUR RELATIONSHIP, Joy invited her parents, my parents, and me over for dinner. Together we prepared this healthful and spicy dish. It's tasty, fun, and romantic.

Indonesian Chicken with Green Beans

Ingredients
6 boned and skinned chicken breasts
½ cup unbleached white flour
¼ teaspoon red pepper powder
¼ teaspoon freshly ground black pepper
½ teaspoon salt (optional)
1 pound fresh or frozen cut green beans
10 cloves garlic minced
1 tablespoon minced gingerroot
1 medium onion, chopped
1 teaspoon olive oil
1 lime, juiced
1 tbsp double black soy sauce (available in oriental food
    stores or make your own by mixing 2 teaspoons soy
    sauce with 1 teaspoon molasses)

---

2 teaspoons brown sugar
2 teaspoons turmeric
½ teaspoon salt (optional)
½ cup water

Directions
1. Preheat oven to 375 degrees.
2. Shake chicken in a plastic bag with flour, red pepper, black pepper, and ½ teaspoon salt until completely coated. Place chicken in a single layer in a baking pan and bake until cooked, about 20 to 30 minutes. Set aside. (You may bake the chicken the night before and refrigerate it until ready to add to sauce.)
3. Steam green beans until tender but still crisp and set aside.
4. Cut chicken into bite-size pieces. Sauté garlic, gingerroot, and onion in olive oil until soft. Add lime juice, soy sauce, brown sugar, turmeric, ½ teaspoon salt, and ¼ cup of the water. Slowly add remaining water, if necessary. Sauce should not be watery. Add chicken and green beans and stir until completely covered with sauce. Serve over rice.

(Adapted from *Choose to Lose* by Dr. Ron Goor & Nancy Goor.)

Chicken Cacciatore

Kevin

◡

HERE IS AN EASY AND TASTY romantic recipe to prepare once
you've invited that special someone to dinner.

Chicken Cacciatore Napoleonville

Ingredients
½ cup chopped celery
1 cup chopped onions
½ cup chopped bell pepper
3 cloves chopped garlic
½ teaspoon salt
¼ teaspoon black pepper
⅛ teaspoon cayenne pepper
1 teaspoon Italian seasoning
2 pounds chicken parts (mixture legs,
    thighs, and breasts)
1 tablespoon margarine or butter
1 can Italian tomatoes
1 can tomato sauce
1 cup red wine
1 bag egg noodles
Parmesan cheese for sprinkling

Directions
1. Chop vegetables and set aside.
2. In a bowl, combine seasonings. Thoroughly rub ½ of the seasoning mix on the chicken parts.
3. In a saucepan, melt margarine at high heat. Add the chicken to the saucepan and sauté until light brown. Remove from pan and set aside.
4. Reduce heat to medium. Add vegetables and remaining seasoning; sauté until light brown. Add tomatoes and tomato sauce. Reduce heat to medium/low and bring to a simmer. Return the chicken to the pan. Add wine and blend well. Cook for 45 minutes stirring occasionally.
5. Prepare noodles per instructions on the package. Serve cacciatore over noodles and sprinkle with Parmesan cheese.

Stir-Fried Beef and Bok Choy

Kevin

~

I REALLY ENJOY THIS RECIPE. It's light and tasty and can be made very spicy or in a "low heat" version. Joy will occasionally surprise me with it for dinner.

Stir-Fried Beef and Bok Choy

Sauce:
1 cup defatted chicken stock
½ cup low-sodium soy sauce
2 tablespoons sugar
1 tablespoon white vinegar
1 tablespoon cornstarch
2 teaspoons chili paste with garlic (can be found in the Asian-products section of some supermarkets)
1 teaspoon sesame oil

Main Dish:
1 pound flank, skirt, or lean sirloin steak
1 pound bok choy (3 cups sliced)
8 scallions
1 teaspoon canola oil
4 medium cloves garlic, crushed through a press

1 small piece fresh ginger, chopped (about 1 tablespoon)
2 medium yellow, red, or green bell peppers,
    sliced (about 2 cups)
2 cups cooked noodles

Directions

1. To make the sauce, mix all ingredients together.
2. To make the Beef and Bok Choy, remove fat from beef. Slice into ½-inch-wide strips 2 to 3 inches long.
3. Wash and dry bok choy. Slice on the diagonal into 1-inch pieces. Slice scallions on the diagonal.
4. Heat the wok and add oil. Add half the garlic and half the ginger and fry until golden, about 30 seconds. Add bok choy, scallions, and peppers and stir-fry until wilted, but still crunchy, about 2 minutes. Remove to a warm serving plate. Add remaining garlic and ginger and stir-fry until golden, about 30 seconds.
5. Add beef and stir-fry for 2 minutes. Remove to plate with vegetables. Add sauce to wok and stir-fry to prevent lumping. Heat until sauce bubbles. Add vegetables and beef to sauce and toss several times. Remove wok from heat. Spoon over noodles and serve immediately.

Teriyaki Fondue

Joy

~

THIS IS A GREAT RECIPE to impress a date with your cooking, and very easy. Plus you get to share the cooking, and you'll have plenty of time to talk in between bites.

Teriyaki Fondue

Ingredients
1½-pound fillet steak or chicken
2 teaspoons light soft brown sugar
¼ cup soy sauce
6 tablespoons dry sherry
2 cloves garlic crushed
1 teaspoon ground ginger

Directions
1. Cut meat into kabob chunks (1-inch cubes). In a large bowl combine sugar, soy sauce, sherry, garlic, and ginger. Pour over meat and leave to marinate for 1 hour or more. A sealable bag works well. Refrigerate about 30 minutes before cooking.
2. Arrange cubes of meat on a platter. Use a fondue pot that is cast iron, enameled metal, or other metal suitable for heating oil. Put oil in pot, filling no more than ⅓ full, or to a depth of 3 inches. Heat to 375 degrees.

3. Spear a cube of meat with a fondue fork and hold it in the hot oil until cooked, about 1 to 2 minutes. Remove from the fondue fork and put on a plate, use a different fork for eating!

‏‏‎ ‎

Serve with a few sauces for dipping,
such as sour cream and chives, mustard mayonnaise,
or sour cream and horseradish.

Portuguese Fish

Kevin

~

ONE OF OUR PREFERRED PLACES to vacation is Provincetown on the tip of Cape Cod. The beaches are good and the food is great, especially the fresh seafood. The Portuguese influence on the cape makes for some marvelous ethnic dishes on the menus in local restaurants.

My sister, Kathy, lives there with her husband, Chris, so Joy and I always have a place to stay. I've been going for so many years that I feel right at home. I also know that we'll eat well when we're there since Chris is an awesome chef. One of my favorite dishes at the Lobster Pot where he works is the Portuguese Fish.

Portuguese Fish

Stuffing:
1 ounce butter, melted
¾ ounce carrot, diced small
¾ ounce onion, diced small
¾ ounce celery, diced small
½ pint sherry
6 ounces mushrooms, sliced
1 teaspoon basil
⅜ teaspoon oregano
⅜ teaspoon thyme

⅛ teaspoon garlic powder
⅛ teaspoon black pepper
12 ounces bread crumbs
1–2 eggs, optional

Directions
Melt butter and sauté the carrot, onion, and celery until mostly cooked. Add sherry and mushrooms. Cook 5 more minutes on high heat. Add seasonings and stir in. Fold in bread crumbs. If you want to bind the stuffing more, add one or two whole eggs.

Sauce:
1 ounce peanut oil
1 tablespoon garlic, minced
½ pound onions, diced medium
½ tablespoon basil
⅜ tablespoon oregano
¼ tablespoon thyme
1 cup rose wine
2¼ cups whole peeled tomatoes, hand crushed

Directions
In a large pot, heat the oil and sauté the garlic and onions. When the onions are translucent, season them and add the wine. Reduce the wine by half. Add tomatoes.

Fish:
Stuffing (see above)
Sauce (see above)
1 ounce bay scallops
1 ounce baby shrimp
1 ounce crabmeat

2 ounces butter
14 ounces codfish
Pinch cumin seeds, ground
1 ounce Bermuda onion, sliced very thin

Directions
1. Make stuffing and pico sauce according to recipes above.
2. In a small sauté pan, cook the scallops, shrimp, and crab in 1 ounce of the butter. (Cook seafood only halfway.) Then mix it into the stuffing.
3. In a casserole, place the codfish on top of the stuffing. Season with cumin and then place the onion on the fish. Pour the remaining butter over the fish and bake at 350 degrees for 20 to 25 minutes. Pour warm Pico sauce on fish and continue baking for 10 to 15 minutes more.

Scallop or Shrimp Creole

Joy

~

KEVIN AND I ATTENDED CLASSES at the New Orleans School of Cooking where we learned that all good Cajun dishes start with the "trinity" of green peppers, onions, and celery. This dish is no exception and is one of my favorites. It's high in taste and low in fat. For a variation, you can replace the scallops and shrimp with a firm white meat fish, such as cod, and cook just a little longer at the end.

Scallop or Shrimp Creole

Ingredients
1 chopped green pepper
1 cup chopped onion
½ cup chopped celery
3 cloves garlic, minced
1½ tablespoons olive oil
1 teaspoon brown sugar
¼ teaspoon freshly ground pepper
½ teaspoon thyme
¼ teaspoon cayenne pepper
1 bay leaf
2 cans tomatoes, drained, juiced, and chopped
1½ cups sliced mushrooms
3 tablespoons chopped parsley

---

1 pound bay scallops or shrimp, shelled and de-veined
2 cups cooked rice

Directions
1. Sauté green pepper, onion, celery, and garlic in olive oil until soft. Add brown sugar, pepper, thyme, cayenne pepper, bay leaf, and stir well. Stir in tomatoes and cook over low heat for 30 minutes or until sauce is thick. Add the mushrooms and cook for a few minutes more.
2. Mix in parsley and shrimp or scallops. Cook for approximately 5 minutes more, until the shellfish is cooked through. Serve immediately to prevent the shellfish from overcooking. Serve over rice.

Peaches and Cream
Cheesecake

Kevin

~

I'M NOT USUALLY A DESSERT EATER, but I helped myself to a
second serving of this at our friend Kendrea's house. We've
modified her recipe slightly and it still tastes great. Try it for a
change of pace when you're making dinner. We hope you'll love
it as much as we do.

Peaches and Cream Cheesecake

Ingredients
¾ cup flour
1 teaspoon baking powder
Salt
1 (3 ⅛ ounce) box vanilla pudding mix, not instant
3 tablespoons butter
1 egg
½ cup whole or 2% milk
1 (1-pound) can sliced peaches, well drained,
      reserving juice
8 ounces cream cheese
½ cup sugar
4 tablespoons reserved peach juice
½ teaspoon cinnamon

Directions
1. Preheat oven to 350 degrees. Grease bottom and sides of a 9 or 10 inch pie plate
2. Combine flour, baking powder, salt, pudding mix, butter, egg, and milk into a mixing bowl. Beat for 2 minutes at medium speed. Pour into prepared pie plate and place drained peaches over the batter.
3. Combine cream cheese, ¼ cup sugar, and peach juice. Beat for 2 minutes at medium speed. Spoon to within 1 inch of edges of pie plate.
4. Combine 1 tablespoon sugar and cinnamon and sprinkle over top. Bake for 30 to 35 minutes or until crust is golden (filling will appear soft). Chill until filling firms.

Rice Krispie Treats
(Wrap It Up!)

Kevin

∽

TONIGHT JOY MADE RICE KRISPIE TREATS. Then she added her own special romantic touch. First she cut them into hearts instead of squares. It takes a little practice and they ended up really cool looking. She wrapped them in Rose colored Reynolds Plastic wrap and served them to me with a big glass of milk, my favorite. I gave her a big hug and a kiss to reward her for my special treats. If your partner doesn't like Rice Krispie Treats, you can do this with brownies, cake, fudge, or any other treat that you slice to serve. Treat your mate to rose hearts; we've even provided the recipe below.

Rice Krispie Treats Recipe

Ingredients
3 tablespoons butter or margarine
6 cups Rice Krispies
1 (10-ounce) bag of marshmallows

Directions
Melt the butter in a large pot over low heat. Stir in the marshmallows until melted. Remove from heat. Stir in the Rice Krispies. Press out the mixture in a 9" x 13" baking pan (use a buttered spatula to prevent sticking). Let cool before slicing. Slice into hearts and wrap with rose colored wrap.

Brigadeiros

Joy

〜

DURING THE HOLIDAYS, Kevin and I like to spend a little time in the kitchen together. One of my favorite memories from growing up in Brazil was making and eating brigadeiros (brig-a-DAY-ros). Brigadeiros are little chocolate caramel candies that are a staple of Brazilian parties. The recipe is simple.

Brigadeiros

Ingredients
2 tablespoons margarine or butter
1 can sweetened condensed milk
2 tablespoons chocolate powder
1 cup of cool water (for texture testing)
Butter or margarine to coat your hands
    (for candy-rolling)
Nonpareils or chocolate sprinkles (for coating
    your candies)

〜

Before you start, plan your stirring rotation.
Making brigadieros requires a lot of stirring, and
switching off will make the task easier for both of you.

---

1. In a medium saucepan, melt the margarine over low heat. Slowly add the condensed milk and keep stirring. Now stir in the chocolate powder. After a while the mixture will begin to thicken; keep stirring. (Your goal is to create a texture that is still soft but when cooled will roll into little balls.)

2. When the mixture starts to boil you're almost there; keep stirring. Shortly after the bubbling begins drop a small amount of the chocolate mixture into the cup of cool water. If you are able to form it into a ball with your fingers it's ready. If it does not form a ball or if it dissolves, keep stirring and try again in another minute or so with a fresh cup of water. This is the only tricky part. If you take the pan off the stove too soon, the candy will be too sticky. If you wait too long, it will crumble. You want it just in between. Once you can make your little ball remove the pan from the heat and allow it to cool until you can handle the chocolate with your fingers.

3. Coat your hands well with the butter or margarine, take a tablespoon of the mixture at a time and roll it into a ball. Once you have formed the balls, roll them in the nonpareils or sprinkles to coat, and put them in candy cups to serve. (The best way to store and serve your brigadeiros is in paper or foil cups, the smallest you can find. They look like miniature cupcake cups.)

It took us a little while to work out a rolling system, but once we got the hang of it, we were brigadeiro pros.

The finished product is delicious, and pretty enough for a party, even if it's a party of two! The romantic part is sharing the work of stirring and rolling. Licking each other's sticky chocolate covered fingers is optional!

To Be Continued

Kevin and Joy

~

THANK YOU FOR JOINING US on this portion of our romantic journey. Reviewing our relationship for this book has reminded us how much fun we're having. We're sure you will find something here to help you kindle, or rekindle, your own romantic relationship. Remember:

- Do the little things that put romance into your everyday life.
- Be creative; use our ideas as they are or as inspiration for your own imagination.
- It doesn't have to be expensive to be memorable.
- If you do have the chance to be fancy or expensive, go for it.
- It can be hard work, but the rewards are worth it!

Please let us know about your successes; we're always looking for new ways to be romantic. Send us your stories via e-mail and maybe we will publish them in our next book!

Kevin and Joy Decker
3016 Talking Rock Dr
Fairfax, VA 22031
ideas@inspirationpoint.com

Bibliography

~

Coleman, Lyman. *Beginnings: Six Lessons to Become a Support Group.* (Littleton: Serendipity House, Inc., 1987)

Guttenberg, Leslie. "Coaching Your Partner." *Pros N' Hackers* June 2002: 6.

Jaffe, Azriela. *Honey, I Want to Start My Own Business.* (New York: HarperCollins Publishers, Inc., 1996)

Lohr, Dick. *Taking Control of Your Time and Your Life.* (Boulder: CareerTrack, Inc., 1995)

Nixon, Richard Gilly. *The Lazy Man's Way to Riches.* (New York: Penguin Books, 1993)

Buckets of Love Contest (1997, December) Retrieved from *www.kfc.com/kfcnews/lsecrets.htm*

DeLaney, Chuck (1999, February) *Romantic Valentine Portraits.* Retrieved from Web site of New York Institute of Photography: *www.nyip.com*

Staying Power (1999, August) Retrieved from *www.proflowers.com/stayingpower*

Appendix

~

Adventure Travel ~ *www.gorp.com, www.backroads.com, www.iexplore.com, www.nps.gov* (National Park Service)

Ballooning ~ *www.bfa.net, www.blastvalve.com*

Bed and Breakfast ~ *www.bbonline.com*

Coupons ~ *www.rom101.com/lovecoupons.htm, www.romancetips.com/coupons*

DRIPs/Stocks ~ *www.dripcentral.com, www.oneshare.com, www.sharebuilder.com, www.frameastock.com, www.buyandhold.com*

Dry Ice ~ *www.dryiceinfo.com*

Flamingos ~ *www.flamingosurprise.com, www.ospsitecrafters.com*

Flowers ~ *www.proflowers.com, 1800flowers.com, www.virtualflowers.com*

Fondue ~ *www.meltingpot.com*

Foot Massage ~ *www.foot.com/html/foot_massage.html, www.massagefree.com/footmassage.html*

Ice Cream ~ *www.benjerry.com*

InspirationPoint ~ *www.inspirationpoint.com*

Kites ~ *www.aka.kite.org, www.kitefestival.org*

Lobster Pot Restaurant ~ *www.ptownlobsterpot.com*

New Orleans Cooking School
~ *www.thelouisianageneralstore.com*

PAIRS ~ *www.pairs.org*

Paving Stones ~ *www.sentsationalbeginnings.com* (search on pathway), *www.hearthsong.com*

Personal Chef ~ *www.hireachef.com*

Personalized Phone Card ~ *www.prepaidphonecardusa.com,*
www.redskies.com

Personalized Romance Novels ~ *www.yournovel.com,*
www.bookbyyou.com, www.paradiseworks-inc.com

Photo Credit Card ~ *www.creditcardfactory.com*

Photography ~ *www.nyip.com, www.thephotosafe.com*

Postmarks ~ *www.loveland.org/valentine,*
www.heartcity.com/vday/cachet.shtml

Songs ~ *www.azlyrics.com*

Special Days ~ *www.holidays.net*

State Parks ~ *www.parksonline.org/stateparks.html*

Tea ~ *www.teamuse.com, www.stashtea.com*

Teddy Bears ~ *www.vermontteddybear.com,*
www.bogiebears.com, www.buildabear.com

Time Capsule ~ *www.futurepkg.com,*
www.affordabletimecapsules.com

Train ~ *www.Amtrak.com*

TV Turnoff Week ~ *www.tvturnoff.org*

Virtual Cards ~ *www.bluemountain.com,*
www.123greetings.com, www.americangreetings.com,
www.greetings.yahoo.com

Volunteering ~ *www.pointsoflight.org*

Web Site Builders ~ *www.geocities.com, www.angelfire.com,*
www.tripod.com